2023中国饭店业务统计
2023 CHINA HOTEL INDUSTRY STUDY

2022 财政年度　FINANCIAL YEAR 2022

中国旅游饭店业协会
China Tourist Hotel Association

浩华管理顾问公司
Horwath HTL

主　　编　　李　峰
副 主 编　　辛　涛　戴雪英
执行副主编　　李芝惠　骆　璿　田思婷
数据汇总　　程　鸣

Editor in Chief　Mr. Li Feng
Executive Editors　Ms. Xin Tao
Ms. Dai Xueying
Associate Editors　Ms. Li Zhihui
Ms. Luo Xuan
Ms. Tian Siting
Data Administration　Mr. Cheng Ming

中国旅游出版社
China Travel & Tourism Press

前言 - FOREWORD

李峰 会长
中国旅游饭店业协会
Li Feng, Chairman
China Tourist Hotel Association

2022 年对中国酒店业来说是极具挑战性的一年。疫情延宕、变乱交织的国际大环境下，酒店业经受了前所未有的严峻冲击。感谢各位同仁在此艰难时刻也怀揣开放心态和分享精神，让社会各界了解到在疫情以来最为艰难的一年中酒店行业的低迷与自救。在此，我谨代表协会感谢各大酒店管理集团与参与问卷回复的 1,570 家酒店的鼎力支持与协助！

2022 年是新冠疫情防控政策进行重大调整的一年，也是大疫三年以来行业的低谷期。2022 年开局，国内多地新冠病例史无前例增加，2021 年所奠定的复苏主基调也被持续多轮的突发性疫情打破。我们看到 2022 年大部分地区的各层级酒店的关键性指标较 2021 年均显著下滑，过去两年表现亮眼的目的地度假酒店市场也增长乏力，业绩一度回落。

值得欣喜的是，在本刊物截稿之际，新型冠状病毒感染已正式归为“乙类乙管”，防疫政策全面调整后，沉寂多时的商务差旅和旅游活动日渐活跃，各地酒店也在端午、五一等小长假期间重现了久违的满房，各行各业的“报复性消费”频频出圈，行业复苏正式迈入快车道。

供给端，“散兵游勇”型酒店的退出催化了行业供需格局的持续优化，投资模式日趋精细，存量市场站上博弈舞台；需求端，在经济发展和疫情催化的双重作用下，消费方式的变革已成定局，酒店从满足基础住宿需求的物业转型成为美好生活方式的载体。具备休闲度假基因、注重人文关怀的城市酒店展现出非同寻常的“常青”魅力。此外，疫情更是让行业认识到降本增效的急迫性，拥抱数字化转型成为高质量发展的重要战略，如何实现科技智能升级的软着陆值得我们深思。

岁聿云暮，一元复始。2023 是复苏之年，更是新一轮征程的开端之年。明者因时而变，知者随事而制——在大转型的时代，保持创新思维和敏锐洞察力，守正创新、与时俱进是从业者应当秉持的精神。我们有理由相信，经此一役，酒店行业不会停下前进的脚步，以专业、精细、创新为核心的长期主义运营思维将成为演绎酒店行业新篇章的主旋律。

The year 2022 was extremely challenging for the hotel sector in China. Indeed, protracted pandemics and volatile political and economic circumstances have a negative impact on hotels. We would like to convey our gratitude to all of our industry friends who, in the face of difficulties, maintained an open mind and a spirit of cooperation. In the most difficult year since the pandemic's outbreak, this enabled society to comprehend the industry's challenges and self-rescue techniques. I want to express my gratitude to the Honorary Board Members and the 1,570 hotels who took part in the survey for their steadfast support and help on behalf of the association!

While the pandemic came to an end in 2022, it also represented the industry's lowest point over these three years. The increases of COVID-19 cases were reported in many regions of the country at the beginning of 2022, upending the recovery trend started in 2021. In most regions, key hotel indicators had declined significantly since 2021, and the destination resort hotel market also experienced sluggish growth and a temporary decline in performance.

It is encouraging to see that COVID-19 is officially classified as a Class B infectious disease at the time of this study's publication. After a comprehensive adjustment of pandemic prevention policies, the business travel and tourism activities, which had been silent for a long time, are gradually resurging. Hotels across the country experienced a long-awaited full occupancy rate during the recent Dragon Boat Festival and May Day holidays. In addition, a number of businesses have seen a common "revenge spending" pattern, suggesting that the industry's recovery has begun to accelerate.

Following the elimination of independent hotels, the supply-demand structure within the sector has experienced continuous optimization. For instance, sophisticated investment models are becoming more dominant. Given the simultaneous effects of economic growth and the pandemic's catalytic effect, the shift in spending patterns on the demand side is now predicted. Hotels are becoming more than just places to stay; they are also ambassadors for a better way of life. Urban hotels with a focus on humanistic care, relaxation, and vacation offer a particularly "evergreen" charm. The industry is now more aware of the value of cost reduction and efficiency improvement as a result of the pandemic's onset. Another important tactic for high-quality development is the adoption of digital transformation. It is worthwhile to consider how to achieve a soft landing of technological intelligence upgrading.

2023 marks the start of a new journey as well as a year of rehabilitation. While the educated adapt to the present, the intelligent change with the times and situations. Practitioners must maintain their original thinking and keen insight while also keeping up with the times in this era of great change. After this disaster, We have reason to believe that the hotel business will continue to grow. The fundamental weapon of this new chapter in the hotel sector will surely be long-term thinking that emphasizes professionalism, refinement, and innovation.

前言 - FOREWORD

戴雪英 执行董事 I 大中华区总经理
浩华管理顾问公司
Julie Dai, Executive Director I General Manager, Greater China
Horwath HTL

在封控、静默中起伏的 2022 年无疑是充满挑战的一年。在 2021 年复苏势头的映衬下，2022 年酒店行业再次受到新冠疫情的猛烈冲击，不分层级、无论地点，各类酒店均面临显著的业绩下滑。但在行业慢行时期，也不乏机遇和亮点涌现，我们希望通过最新一期的《中国饭店业务统计》为各位展现市场的真实情况。

2022 年，全国大部分地区在毫无预兆的疫情暴发之下实行诸多管控措施，中国酒店市场整体业绩再一次跌至谷底。其中，一线城市酒店业绩下挫显著，二、三线市场中，自带休闲气质的城市酒店业绩降幅相对较小。其中，部分应时打造城中休闲体验的五星级酒店业绩水平实现逆跌。而疫情前期大放异彩的目的地度假村市场受到主要客源来源地长时间封控的影响，平均房价和平均住宿率双双下滑，积极势头有所衰减。

客房之外，酒店餐饮需求也再次降到冰点。艰难时期激发了从业者的“求生意志”，除了成本管控外，酒店纷纷以外卖、摊贩销售等形式开拓本地新市场；同时，以月饼等产品为代表的餐饮零售也开始用力“内卷”。在餐饮领域具备持续优势的酒店依托餐饮社区化的理念在新赛道中一往无前，开启了酒店餐饮的二次革命。

2023 年伊始，我们告别了口罩和核酸检测，以休闲度假为首的需求强势复苏，被疫情压抑的会议会展和商旅需求集中释放，也为酒店市场业绩回升按下快进键。按照中国农历计算，2023 年是个双春年，“一年打两春，黄土变为金”，希望各位行业同仁在这双喜的一年谨记疫情期间的奋斗与果敢，在产品端打破陈规，创造提供情绪价值的引领性酒店；在运营端以数字为舵、以服务为帆，迎来行业新的“大航海时代”。

最后，我谨代表浩华管理顾问公司，衷心感谢中国旅游饭店业协会给予本刊物一贯的支持与帮助！也诚挚地感谢荣誉顾问团成员以及参与调查研究的 1,570 家酒店给予本年度刊物的鼎力支持。作为中国酒店业界最权威、最全面、最可靠的数据平台，《中国饭店业务统计》迄今已连续出版 21 年。站在下一个 20 年的起点，希望能与各位业界同仁继续携手共进，迈入行业新征程！

2022 was surely a difficult year, filled with many highs and lows among lockdowns and stillness. Despite the momentum of the recovery in 2021, COVID-19 pandemic struck the hotel industry hard in 2022 once more. Regardless of brand positioning or location, all hotel types experienced significant performance decreases. However, this time of sluggishness also saw the emergence of chances and bright spots. We aim to showcase market dynamics following the pandemic and highlight the significant challenges and opportunities in this most recent issue of China Hotel Industry Study.

Following the abrupt pandemic outbreak in 2022, most parts of the nation undertook various control measures, and the Chinese hotel market once again hit an all-time low. Hotel performance in first-tier cities decreased dramatically, while city hotels with relaxed atmosphere had relatively lesser reductions in second and third-tier markets. Smaller declines were observed in five-star hotels that provide urban leisure experiences, and some even produced better results. The destination resort market, which had thrived in the pre-pandemic era, was impacted by the lengthy lockdowns of its key consumer sources. As a result, there was a fall in occupancy as well as average room rates, and the earlier favorable momentum slowed down.

Beyond guest rooms, the demand for Food & Beverage also dropped to freezing point once again. These challenging times inspired hotel practitioners to harness their survival instincts. Hotels also explored new local markets through delivery and street vendor sales in addition to cost-control initiatives. Meanwhile, F&B retail also started moving forward quickly at this time, including mooncakes and other products. Leading the way in this new trend of catering communityization were hotels with a sustained edge in food and beverage. As a result, they started a second revolution in the hotel F&B industry.

We say goodbye to masks and nucleic acid testing in 2023. A strong rebound was fueled by a high demand for leisure travel. Additionally, previously restrained demand for business trips, conferences, and exhibits was released, which gave the hotel market's performance a quick boost. The year 2023 is a double spring year, or, in the words of the Chinese lunar calendar, "two springs in one year, turning yellow earth into gold." Hoteliers are urged to keep in mind their adversity and bravery throughout the pandemic. In order to embrace the new "century of great exploration" in the sector, they should continue to shatter norms by building cutting-edge hotels that offer emotional value and breaking traditions on the operational side by sailing with service and steering with figures.

Finally, on behalf of Horwath HTL, I would like to express my sincere gratitude to the China Tourist Hotel Association for its ongoing support and cooperation with this publication! Additionally, I would like to express my gratitude to the 1,570 responding hotels and the members of our Honorary Advisory Board for their steadfast support of this year's publication. China Hotel Industry Study has been continually published for 21 years and is the most authoritative, comprehensive, and dependable data platform in the Chinese hotel industry. Standing at the beginning of the next 20 years, we aim to continue collaborating with industry colleagues to embark on a new journey of the industry!

Commentary 2022

For the third consecutive year, the pandemic cast a shadow on the Chinese hotel business in 2022. However, given the decline in virus pathogenicity, foreign nations, unlike the previous two years, gradually loosened their pandemic prevention and control measures. While confirmed cases were at high levels and sporadic outbreaks occurred in various places, first-tier cities like Shanghai and Beijing were under pressure from the risk of imported infections. In the middle of the ups and downs of lockdowns and stillness in 2022, the momentum of the hotel market recovery in 2021 slowly dissipated. The operating performance of the hotel sector dramatically fell in 2022, with certain regions even dropping below the level of 2020.

Despite a general downturn in the business, the hotel market also showed distinct performance swings under several key variables. These statistics might offer us fresh perspectives on how to adjust to the post-pandemic environment.

- Location type: although destination resorts still hold the leading position in RevPAR, they were unable to reproduce the advantages of 2021. The impact of the pandemic lockdowns severely affected the sources of customers, and the occupancy rate of destination resorts even fell to the bottom for all types of locations. Shanghai and Beijing also pulled down the average level of first-tier cities under the impact of prolonged lockdowns, and hotel revenues in first-tier cities were greatly impacted. However, second-tier cities with excellent leisure qualities, represented by Changsha and Hangzhou, have shown relatively stable performance levels.

- Star rating: the pandemic affected hotels of all star ratings. The higher the star rating, the greater the decline in RevPAR and operating margin. The GOPPAR for five-star hotels fell to an all-time low. Operating profit margins continued to be lowest in the four-star sector. Since 2020, it has continuously underperformed the three-star market, and the difference is getting bigger every year.

- Room rate: the decline in GOP ratio is proportional to the average room rate. Hotels with an ADR over 1,000 yuan experienced the most significant decline in GOP ratio, approaching 15 percentage points. These high-priced hotels are mostly located in first-tier cities and key second-tier cities. Due to the unpredictable fluctuations caused by the pandemic in 2022, various types of demand remained low, but operating costs could not be substantially reduced. This caused a significant drop in GOP ratio.

The impact of the pandemic has led to a contraction in business travel and tourism activities, and room revenues have been hit hard. Some practitioners shifted their focus to the F&B sector, which has a shorter radius of radiation. In an effort to generate cash flow for hotels during a downturn through localized and social activities, a variety of new forms—such as takeout and retail—emerged. However, the data demonstrates that, the decline in F&B revenues for hotels at all levels is still significantly higher than room revenues. In the post-pandemic period, streamlining F&B may be a shortcut to guarantee the overall revenue of hotels. However, during the pandemic, hotels' proactive self-rescue showed the potential for F&B reform and innovation in the industry.

2022年概要

2022年是中国酒店行业笼罩在疫情阴霾下的第三年。但与前两年不同的是，随着病毒致病力的下降，海外国家纷纷“躺平”，取消防疫管控措施；而以上海、北京为代表的一线城市不堪疫情输入风险的重压，确诊病例连续高位运行，各地也面临着此起彼伏的散点暴发。2021年酒店市场的复苏势头在2022年封控和静默的起伏中悄然熄灭，2022年酒店行业运行轨迹明显下滑，部分层级和地区甚至无法追平2020年的水平。

尽管行业遭遇整体下行，但是从不同维度来看，酒店市场也展现出了差异化的业绩波动态势，这些数字将给予我们适应后疫情时代的新启示。

- 从地点类型上看，尽管目的地度假酒店仍占据平均每间房收益的领头羊地位，但也难再现2021年一骑绝尘的优势。由于疫情管控，客源受损严重，目的地度假酒店的住宿率甚至跌至各类地点市场末尾。而在长时间封控的波及下，上海、北京也拉低了整体一线城市的平均水平，一线城市酒店收入水平受损严重。以长沙、杭州为代表的具备强休闲气质的二线城市则展现了相对稳定的业绩水平。

- 从定位星级上看，各星级酒店均受到疫情波及。星级越高，平均每间房收益和经营利润率的下跌幅度越大，五星级酒店每间房均摊经营利润遭遇腰斩，达到历史最低值。四星级市场仍是经营利润的洼地，自2020年以来持续低于三星级，且差距逐年拉升。

- 从房价水平上看，经营利润率的下降幅度与平均房价构成正比关系，平均房价在1,000元以上的酒店经营利润率下滑最为显著，接近15个百分点。这类高房价酒店多位于一线城市和重点二线城市，在2022年疫情反复无常的冲击下，各类需求持续低迷，但运营成本难以实现质的突破，因此经营利润率明显下跌。

疫情的冲击导致商务差旅和旅游活动缩水，客房收入遭遇重创，部分从业者将目光转向辐射半径更短的餐饮板块。外卖、零售等花样层出不穷，力求通过在地化和社会化运作为处于低迷期的酒店创造现金流量来源。但从数据来看，各层级酒店的餐饮收入下滑幅度仍明显高于客房收入。后疫情时期，精简餐饮或为保障酒店整体收益的捷径，但疫情期间酒店的积极自救也展现出酒店餐饮改革创新、跑赢大盘的可能性。

Part 1 Leisure demand shows resilience in difficult times

Recovery halts and overall performance falters again

COVID-19 pandemic, the worst worldwide infectious disease outbreak in nearly a century, started in 2020.The hotel business was given a devastating hit, with market performance collapsing dramatically. The pandemic situation was mostly under control in a number of places by 2021, thanks to routine prevention measures and widespread vaccination, and a number of market performance indices demonstrated meaningful signs of recovery. But as the pandemic approached its third year in early 2022, frequent outbreaks in a number of cities crushed expectations of a return to normal. The year was marred by protracted lockdowns and regular nucleic acid testing. Moreover, a collective infection before the complete opening at the end of the year negatively impacted the hotel industry. Meanwhile, the global economy continued to deteriorate as a result of the three-year pandemic, and the international situation remained complicated. hotel market performance hit a historical low in 2022.

The 2022 pandemic episode was distinguished by wider radiation, a longer duration, and stricter control measures as opposed to the dispersed regional breakouts of 2021. As a result, the market as a whole experienced persistently low occupancy. In 2022, the occupancy of five-star hotels was only 43%, which is a truly low record. Three-star and four-star hotel occupancy rates, meanwhile, marginally down to 51% and 45%, respectively. Looking back over the past two years, occupancy was undoubtedly the main statistic that the outbreak had an influence on. While the ADR of four- and five-star hotels also varied in its drop in 2022, the ADR of three-star and limited-service hotels saw a little increase, though they were still below 2019 levels. The RevPAR of four- and five-star hotels fell once more in 2022 under the dual pressure of occupancy and ADR. In fact, the RevPAR for five-star hotels fell by 18%, which is the lowest level in the previous 20 years.

Exhibit 1: RevPAR Performance, by Star Rating, China, 2002-2022

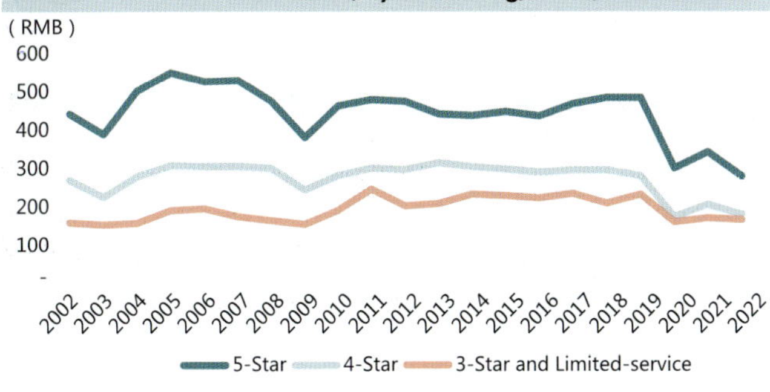

The GOP for the total market was impacted by the declining ADR and occupancy trends. The GOP disparity between hotels with various star ratings shrank and became more concentrated in 2022. The higher the hotel star rating, the more severe the decline in GOP ratio. In 2022, the GOP ratio of five-star hotels nationwide was only 13%. The GOPPAR collapsed, falling even below the pre-pandemic level of three-star and limited-service hotels. Once more, the GOP ratio and GOPPAR of four-star hotels were at the very bottom of the market. Since the pandemic, the GOPPAR of four-star hotels has been consistently lower than that of three-star hotels.

第一部分 休闲需求在困境中展现坚韧特性

复苏戛然而止，整体业绩再次遇冷

2020年，新冠疫情暴发，近百年来全球最严重的传染病大流行拉开了序幕，酒店行业遭受了前所未有的剧烈冲击，国内市场业绩跌至谷底。2021年，得益于常态化防疫和大规模的疫苗接种，各地疫情相对可控，市场各项业绩指标也显著回温。2022年伊始，在疫情进入第三个年头之时，多座主要城市的疫情频发粉碎了酒店业"回归常态"的希望。漫长的封控和频繁的核酸检测成为贯穿全年的阴霾，年终全面放开前的集体感染更是为酒店行业带来了沉重一击。与此同时，世界经济在三年疫情的冲击下持续下行，国际形势变局交织，在多重压力的持续发酵和演化下，2022年酒店市场业绩再次来到历史低点。

不同于2021年零散的区域性复发，2022年的疫情具有辐射更广、时间更长、管控措施更为严格的特性，这也导致整体市场住宿率持续低迷。分层级来看，2022年五星级酒店的平均住宿率仅为43%，跌入真正意义上的"历史谷底"。而三、四星级的住宿率小幅下滑分别至51%和45%的水平。纵观过去两年的市场业绩，住宿率无疑是疫情首要冲击的指标；2022年，四、五星级酒店的平均房价也出现程度不一的下滑；仅三星及有限服务酒店实现了房价的小幅提振，却仍难与2019年的水平相提并论。在平均住宿率和平均房价的双面夹击下，2022年四、五星级酒店市场的平均每间房收益再次跳水，五星级平均每间房收益下跌18%，为过去20年的最低谷。

图1：2002年至2022年各定位层级酒店市场平均每间房收益表现

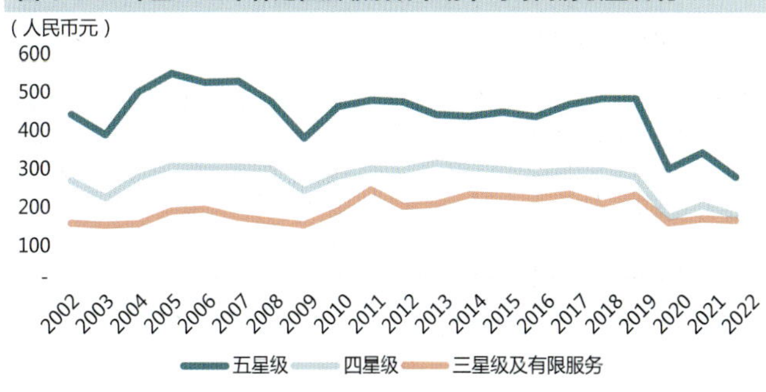

平均房价和平均住宿率的低迷势头同样影响着整体市场的经营毛利。2022年各档次酒店毛利差异缩小，集中于低位。而星级越高的酒店，经营毛利率下跌程度越严重——2022年全国五星级酒店的平均经营毛利率仅为13%，每间可供房均摊经营毛利惨遭腰斩，甚至不及疫情前三星及有限服务酒店的水平。四星级酒店的经营毛利率和每间可供房经营毛利再次居于市场末位。自疫情以来，四星级酒店的每间可供房经营毛利持续低于三星及有限服务酒店，且差距逐年拉大，可谓举步维艰。

Exhibit 2: GOP Ratio Comparison, by Star Rating, 2021/2022

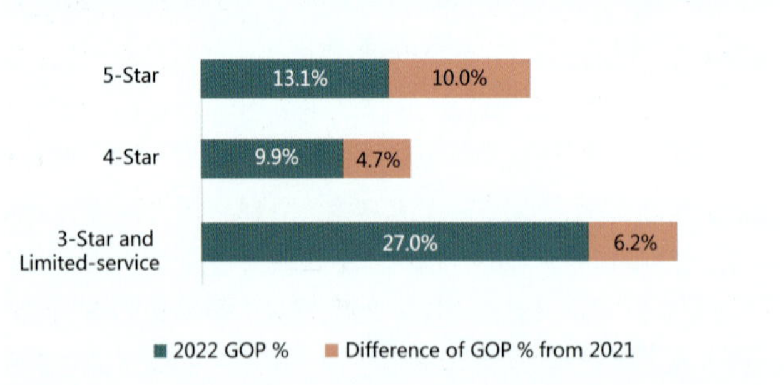

Tourist destinations still shine but with a subdued glow

When comparing different city tiers, first-tier cities enjoy the general market rebound with a significant increase in occupancy as well as the benefits of their high population density and high mobility. But this also set the tone for the countless lockdowns that followed periodic pandemic breakouts. The most serious harm occurred to first-tier cities in 2022 as a result of the total lockdown in Shanghai from the end of March to June, the stringent control of the Winter Olympics in Beijing in February, and ongoing regional closures throughout the year. The RevPAR was dragged down by a significant contraction in occupancy, down by 12 percentage points compared to 2021, replicating the dismal picture of 2020. In contrast, hotels in second- and third-tier cities benefited from the "dual circulation" and "unified large market" policies. They thus experienced a relatively smaller decline in occupancy rates in 2022, with approximate 4 to 5 percentage points drop, and basically maintained stable customer sources.

The market for vacation resorts had been booming during the first two years of pandemic. In 2022, it experienced its first setback. While its RevPAR remained the highest of the four location areas, its ADR underperformed the other three, falling by 7 percentage points. On the other hand, the destination market's ADR decline did not lead to sustained occupancy. Multiple lockdowns caused severe harm to the long-haul destination customer base, and the Shanghai pandemic significantly reduced the performance of suburban destinations in the Yangtze River Delta. Second only to first-tier cities, the occupancy of the entire tourist destination market fell by over 6 percentage points.

Exhibit 3：5-Star Hotels' Market Performance Comparison, by City Tier and Tourism Destination, 2022

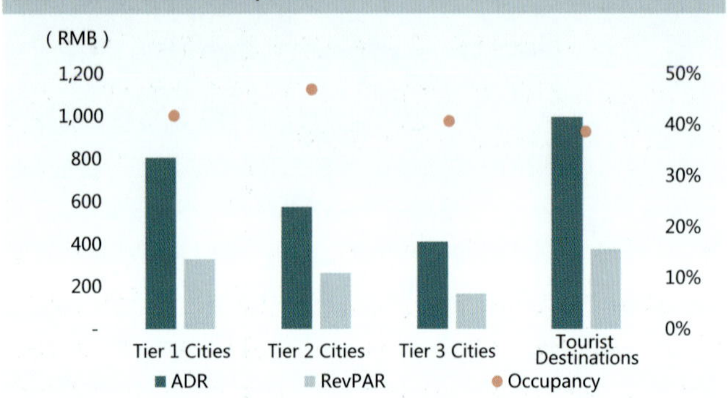

图2：2022年与2021年各定位层级酒店市场经营利润率变化表现

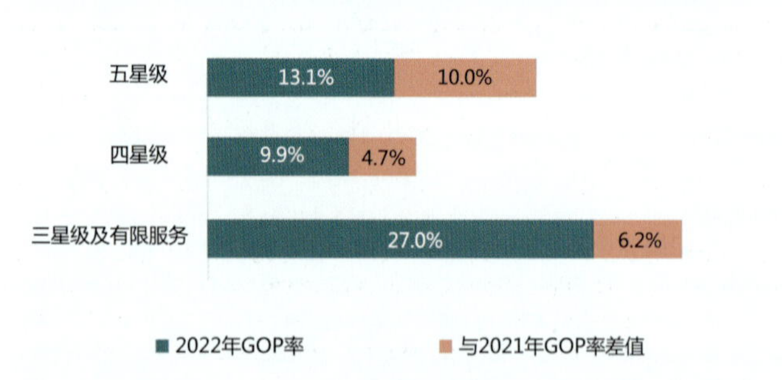

旅游目的地光彩未尽，但稍显黯淡

分城市层级来看，一线城市人口密度高、流动性强的特征赋予了其在整体市场复苏之际，住宿率强势回升的优势，但也奠定了它在疫情防控政策调整前灰暗的主基调。2022年，上海自3月底至6月的整体封控、北京2月冬奥会的严格管理以及全年接连不断的区域性封闭，使一线城市酒店市场在2022年受损最为严重，平均每间房收益被平均住宿率的大幅缩水所拖累，相比2021年降幅达12个百分点，复刻了2020年的惨淡景象。相较而言，受益于"双循环"和"统一大市场"政策的二、三线城市酒店，其住宿率在2022年跌幅相对较小，控制在4至5个百分点区间内，客源基本维稳。

在疫情前两年大放异彩的目的地度假市场却在2022年遭遇了疫情以来的首次滑铁卢。尽管平均每间房收益仍居四类地点市场之首，但平均房价跌幅却达到7个百分点，超过其他三个地点市场；并且目的地市场平均房价的下滑并未成功换取平均住宿率的平稳。在疫情多轮防控之下，长线目的地客源基础受损严重；上海的疫情也显著拉低了长三角区域近郊度假胜地的业绩水平，整体旅游目的地市场住宿率一路下滑超6个百分点，跌幅仅次于一线城市。

图3：2022年各层级城市及目的地度假市场五星级酒店核心经营业绩比较

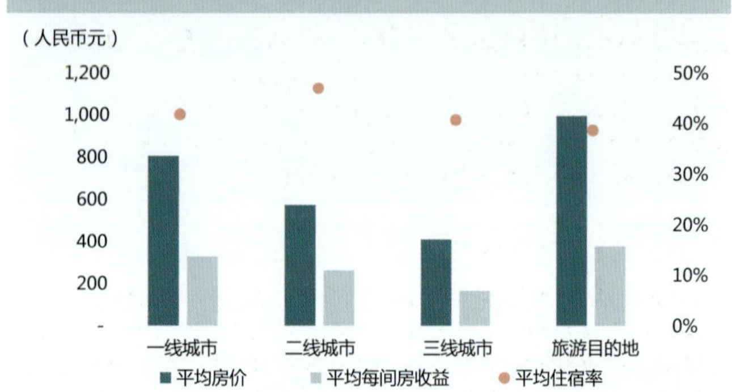

Sanya, the market leader in the destination resort, benefited from the return of high-end domestic customers under the pandemic, as well as the gathering of high-quality vacation products. Its performance had increased instead of decreasing during the first two years of the pandemic. However, in 2022, Sanya, a significant player, also faded out of the spotlight. Although its performance level still ranked first among key cities, with an GOPPAR exceeding 75% of the second-ranked Guangzhou, and the RevPAR was nearly twice that of the four first-tier cities, compared to its own performance, the GOPPAR of Sanya has fallen to the pre-pandemic level, even below that of 2019. As a market that relies significantly on individual travelers, Sanya's main customer base was affected due to recurrent lockdowns in the key customer source locations, which were based on first-tier cities. Furthermore, the local pandemic that broke out in Sanya in August, the traditional peak season, forced many tourists to stay, and the advantage of the peak season was lost, which negatively affected the overall performance of the Sanya market in 2022.

Exhibit 4: 5-Star Hotels' GOPPAR and RevPAR Comparison, Tier 1 Cities, 2022

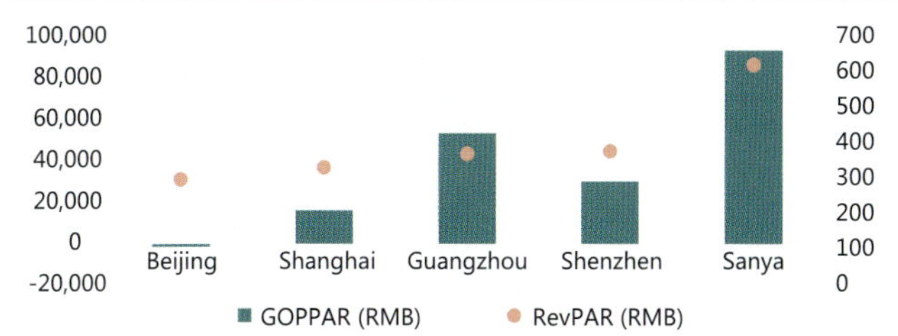

Exhibit 5: 5-Star Hotels' GOPPAR and RevPAR Comparison, Sanya, 2018-2022

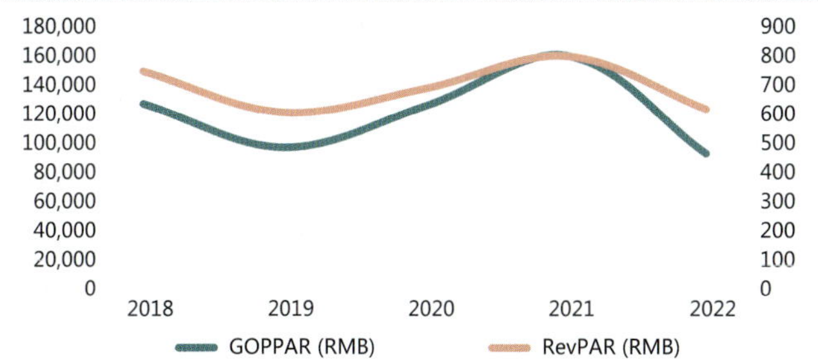

Consumer travel options are no longer restricted to domestic holiday spots once national borders reopened in 2023. However, the consuming habits that developed over the course of the pandemic's three-year duration won't shift suddenly. Additionally, the erratic epidemic and international political conditions continue to worry consumers. As a result, over time, their acceptance of international travel will gradually increase. Given that outbound tourism has not yet recovered, there is reason to think that remote locations like Sanya can continue to operate at reasonably constant performance levels in the near future.

City marketing and leisure atmosphere remain crucial for success

Given the effects of various pandemic outbreaks in various regions, an examination of the performance of 5-star hotels in China's major cities in 2022 clearly reveals the endurance of the "strong south, weak north" pattern. Only Jinan and Qingdao in the north benefited from the lighter regulatory measures in Shandong Province. They moved into the top

目的地度假村市场中的鳌头——三亚，受益于疫情之下国内出境客群的回流，加之本身优质度假产品的聚集，在疫情前两年业绩不降反增。然而在2022年的魔幻剧情下，唱足主角戏份的三亚也从聚光灯下淡出。尽管业绩水平仍高居重点城市榜首，每间可供房均摊经营毛利超过第二名广州75%，平均每间房收益也是四个一线城市的近2倍；但同比自身，三亚的每间可供房经营毛利已经跌落至疫情前水平，甚至低于2019年。对于以旅游散客为绝对主力的市场，一线城市等主要客源地的严格疫情防控导致三亚支柱客群的缺席；此外，三亚在传统旺季8月暴发的本地疫情迫使大量游客滞留，旺季优势不再，也直接拉低了2022年三亚市场的整体业绩表现。

图4：2022年一线城市五星级酒店每间可供房经营利润和平均每间房收益比较

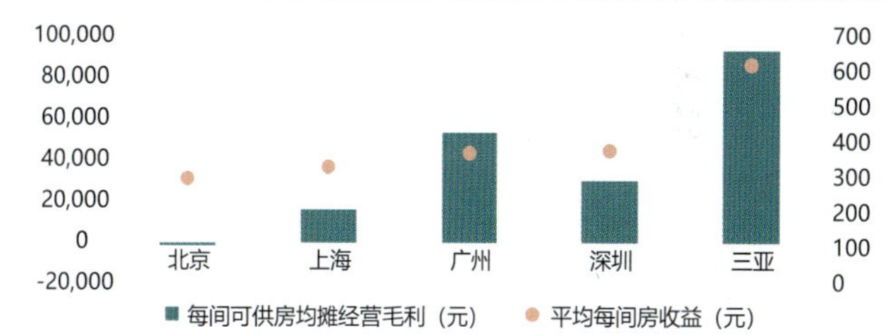

图5：2018年至2022年三亚五星级酒店每间可供房经营利润和平均每间房收益

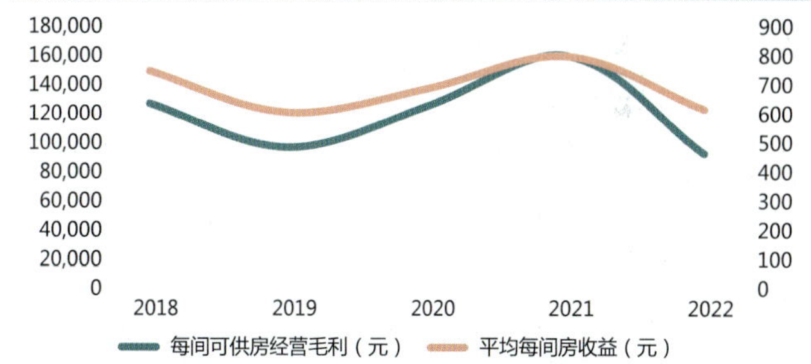

尽管2023年国门打开，消费者的旅游选择不再局限于国内度假目的地，但是，疫情三年所养成的消费习惯并不会在一夕之间改变，加之对境外不稳定的疫情及政治因素心存顾虑，消费者对于境外旅游的接纳程度仍待循序渐进。我们有理由相信，在短期内，以三亚为代表的远程目的地仍可借着出境旅游尚未完全恢复之机维持较为稳定的业绩水平。

城市营销+休闲气质仍是王道

回顾2022年中国重点城市五星级酒店的业绩水平不难发现，受到疫情多次、多地暴发的影响，2020年全国各地住宿率均显著下滑，但南强北弱的格局依旧存在。北方城市中，仅济南和青岛得益于山东省相对宽松的管控政策，闯入重点城市五星级酒店

ten of 5-star hotels occupancy in key cities. Aside from the three first-tier cities, second-tier cities in the south with a distinct leisure lifestyle, like Changsha and Hangzhou, performed better in terms of RevPAR and were rated second and fourth, respectively, nationwide.

Exhibit 6: 5-Star Hotels' Market Performance Comparison, by Key Cities, 2022

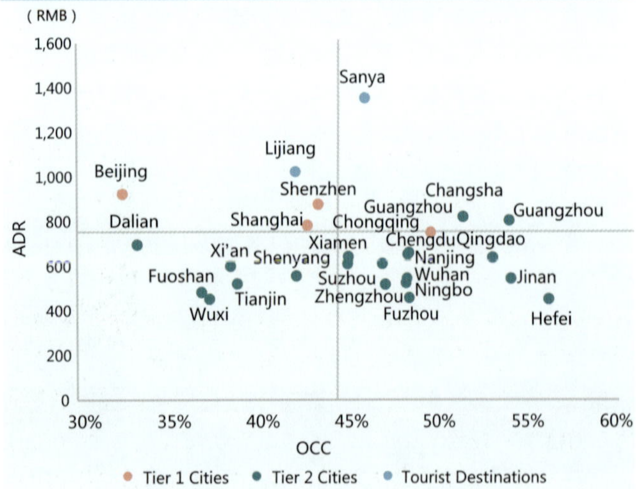

Its reputation as the "entertainment capital," along with well-known landmarks like Hunan Satellite TV and food-related IPs like Wenheyou, helped Changsha, a leading city with an abundance of urban communication resources, become a must-visit destination for young consumers. Despite the pandemic's effects, Changsha's occupancy only decreased by 10 percentage points in 2022 compared to 2019 because of the city's great appeal to younger generations. New-generation hotel products have entered the market as a result of this popularity boom. Among the top five hotels in Changsha, the ADR of 5-star hotels increased by more than 26% and surpassed RMB 1,000.

Exhibit 7: Performance Changes of Top 5 Five-star Hotels in Changsha in RevPAR, 2019/2022

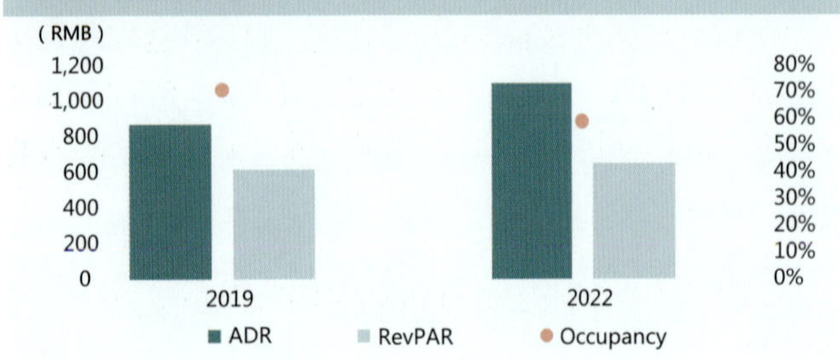

Hangzhou is another "Evergreen Tree" in the 5-star market. During the pandemic, its robust performance was a clear reflection of the local trend of "staycation" and leisure vacation in the hotel industry. In 2022, frequent regional changes in pandemic prevention and control measures made traveling a luxurious expectation. However, desire for leisure and vacation remained strong. The pent-up desire for travelling freely that had accumulated over the past three years reached its peak under the strengthened pandemic control measures in 2022. When inter-provincial

住宿率前十。而南方，若刨去3个一线城市，二线城市中休闲气质鲜明的长沙、杭州都实现了较优的平均每间房收益，分别位列全国第二和第四位。

图 6：2022年中国重点城市五星级酒店业绩表现

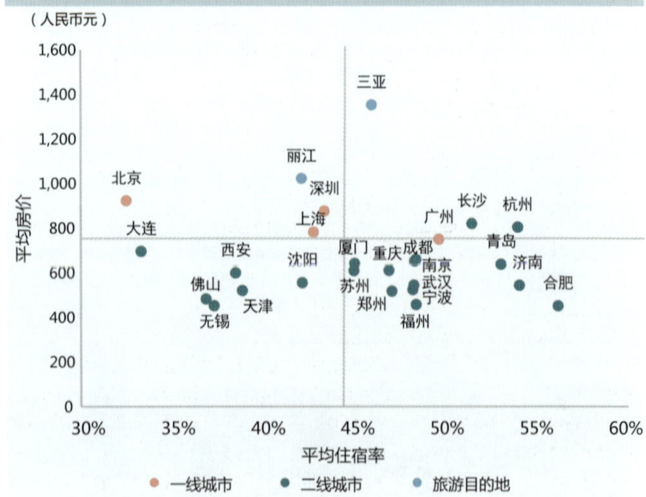

作为老牌顶流制造机，长沙拥有丰富的城市传播资源，除了家喻户晓的湖南卫视，近年来文和友等美食IP也成为必打卡的地标。以娱乐之都为核心的城市营销在疫情期间成功捕获大量年轻消费群体，2022年长沙平均住宿率较2019年相比仅下跌十个百分点。暴涨的人气在疫情期间也加速了新一代酒店产品的入市步伐，推动长沙五星级酒店的平均房价实现跃升。平均每间房收益排名前五的酒店在疫情前后的平均房价涨幅超过26%，一举突破千元大关。

图 7：2022年和2019年长沙五星级酒店平均每间房收益排名前五酒店的业绩变化

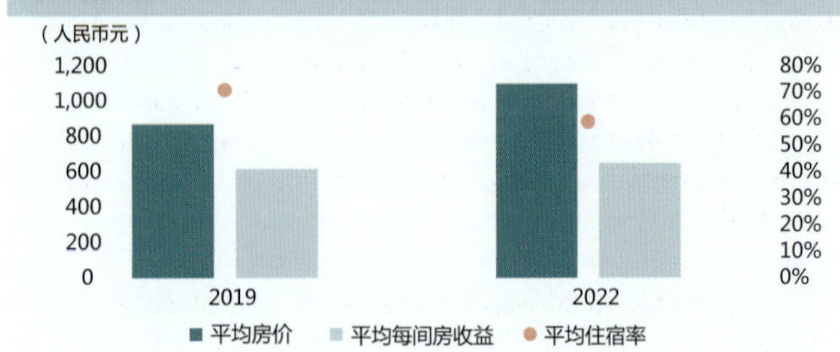

五星级市场的另一棵常青树是杭州。疫情期间，杭州的业绩高企是本地游、宅度假风潮在酒店行业的鲜明体现。2022年，各地频繁变化的疫情防控措施让出门旅游变成了奢望，但是人们休闲度假的渴望却丝毫不减。积压了三年对自由出行的向往在2022年的加强版防疫管控下到达顶峰：跨省游叫停就去近郊，静态管理就留守城市，可谓“没有条件也要创

travel was suspended, people turned to nearby destinations. When static management was enforced, they stayed in the city. People were determined to "create conditions even when there were none," and hotels became their primary base for exploring new experiences in familiar cities.

Unlike traditional business-oriented cities such as Wuhan and Zhengzhou, Hangzhou offers a strong leisure culture, with a mix of traditional attractions and trendy elements. Inspired by the city's DNA, 5-star hotels in Hangzhou created city walk itineraries, themed afternoon teas, cooking workshops with famous chefs, aromatherapy sessions and other leisure activities. They evolved into new types of micro-vacation places, catering to young people seeking a more relaxed attitude to travel and a "staycation" mindset, making themselves ideal for a "hotel gap day."

Although the pandemic has become a thing of the past, the changes brought about by it continue to permeate all aspects of life today. The immersive and experiential consumption trend embodied by "staycations" undoubtedly has a significant impact on the hotel business. On the one hand, the abstract and internalized desire for "experience" raises the bar for hotel design. How to deliver emotional value and sensory experience in limited spaces through components such as local culture, artistic fashion, and natural ecology, while also connecting with the environment and consumers, will be fundamental in future hotel design. On the other hand, the hotel must still explore its own capabilities to stretch and mold as a traditional provider of food and lodging services. By providing its consumers with various “scene” experiences and featured activities outside of sleep, the hotel allows them to truly “experience new sights from a new perspective.”

Part II: Hotel F&B sectors explore new development paths and highlights emerge in the crisis

F&B faces revenue reduction, cost-cutting and revenue-increasing measures become a top priority

Compared to the difficult winter experienced by hotel rooms, the suffering faced by hotel F&B was even greater. In 2022, the decline in F&B revenue for each star-rated sector was significantly greater than that of room revenue. Four-star hotels saw an 18% decrease, twice the room revenue decline. Although the operating hours of various hotel F&B outlets largely returned to their pre-pandemic level, the seat turnover per day plummeted due to the impact of the pandemic. This led to a continuous decline in catering revenue. In 2022, the F&B revenue per available room in four- and five-star hotels was even lower than that in 2020, and contracted by over 40% compared to 2019.

Exhibit 8: F&B Revenue PAR Comparison, by Star Rating, China, 2013–2022

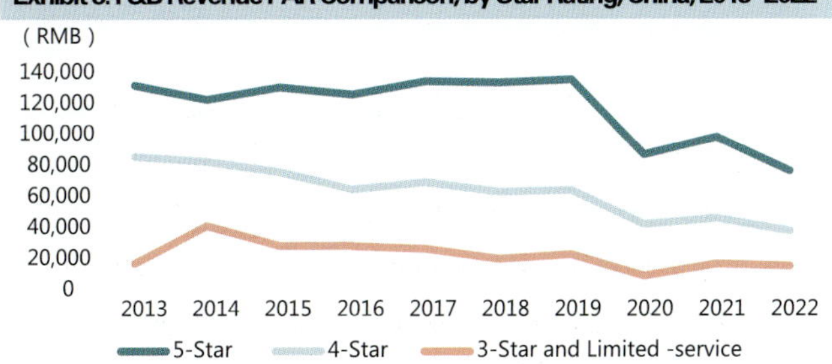

造条件”，酒店便成了人们在熟悉的城市中玩出新意的首要据点。

不同于武汉、郑州等经典商务型城市，杭州休闲氛围浓郁，传统景点和网红元素兼具。在城市基因的引导下，杭州五星级酒店也开启了对生活方式的探索，适时打造城中漫游旅游路线，开发主题下午茶、大厨烹饪课、芳香理疗等各类休闲娱乐活动，摇身一变成为新型微度假目的地，对于当下追求佛系度假、“躺吃式旅行”的年轻人而言，“酒店Gap Day”无疑是最佳选择。

站在当下回望，虽然疫情已成往事，但疫情所带来的变化依然渗透生活的方方面面。宅度假所代表的沉浸式和体验感消费趋势也势必给酒店行业带来深远影响。一方面，“体验”这种抽象的内化需求对酒店设计提出更高要求，如何在有限的空间内以在地文化、艺术时尚、自然生态等元素提供情绪价值、感官体验，与场域形成共鸣、与消费者同频共情，都将成为未来酒店设计的核心课题。另一方面，酒店作为传统提供吃、住服务的载体，仍需挖掘自身延展空间可塑性的能力，通过不同的场景体验、特色活动体验填补睡眠之外的时间空白，让消费者能真正在酒店“换个角度看到全新的风景”。

第二部分　酒店餐饮自救闯新路，危机催生亮点频现

餐厅正常营业，收入几近腰斩，开源节流成头等大事

相比酒店客房所经历的寒冬，酒店餐饮更是一落千丈。与2021年相比，2022年各星级酒店餐饮收入的降幅均明显超过客房收入，其中四星级酒店餐饮收入降幅达18%，甚至为客房收入降幅的两倍。尽管酒店的各类餐厅和宴会的营业时长已基本恢复至疫情前水平，但是每日每餐位平均上座数仍在疫情影响下跌至谷底，餐饮收入也因此一路走低。2022年四、五星级酒店的每间可供房餐饮收入甚至低于2020年水平，与2019年相比更是缩水超过40%。

图8：2013年至2022年各定位层级酒店市场每间可供房餐饮收入

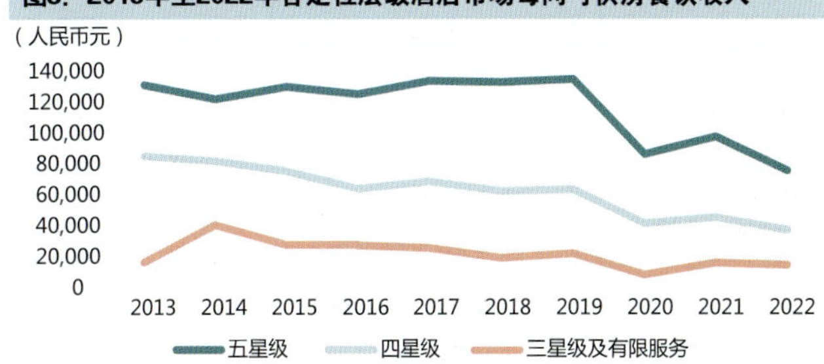

However, hotel F&B managers did not sit idly by, as demonstrated by the reduced F&B expenses. In 2022, F&B expenses per available room in all types of hotels tightened to a certain extent. Among them, the most significant decline of F&B expenses in five-star hotels came from labor costs.

Nonetheless, the impact of the pandemic on hotel F&B, heavily reliant on banquets and business dinners, was still fatal. The unpredictable temporary closures prevented guests from dining in the hotel. During the pandemic, people tended to reduce close contacts, and hotel restaurants added potential contact risks from out-of-town guests compared to social caterings. Therefore, the F&B profits per available room in all types of hotels continued to decline in 2022, with the GOP for three-star hotels almost close to zero.

Exhibit 9: F&B GOP PAR Comparison, by Star Rating, China, 2013–2022

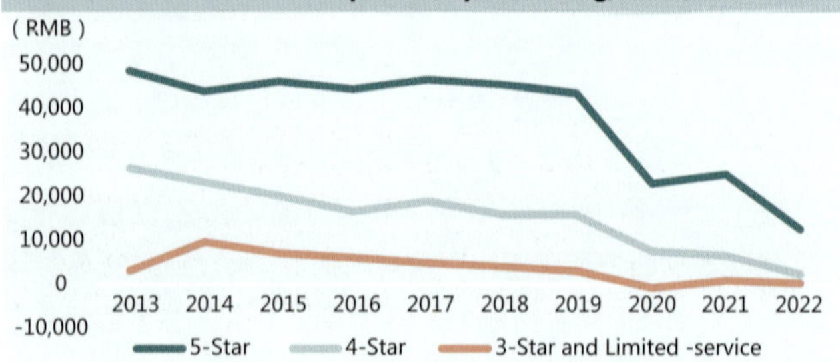

Hotel F&B has attempted to innovate, but the "the strong getting stronger" trend persists.

Despite the significant decline in hotel F&B, the principle of "the strong getting stronger" still applies. Looking at key cities, Guangzhou and Shenzhen still firmly occupy the top two positions in both ADD and Chinese restaurants categories. Thanks to their unique culinary culture, residents in these two cities display a relatively higher level of pursuit of and willingness to pay for hotel dining. In order to secure a foothold in the fiercely competitive catering industry, hotel F&B constantly innovate, not only in terms of meals and offerings, but also in pricing and marketing strategies that resonate with local customers. Several hotel restaurants highly favored among residents have emerged on the market throughout the past few years. As a result, despite the pandemic's impact, local cuisine fans continue to support hotel F&B outlets. In comparison, the seating rates for hotel restaurants in Beijing and Shanghai are less than satisfactory. On the one hand, long-term closures in 2022 severely reduced the utilization rate of dining seats. On the other hand, the expansion of hotel catering in Beijing and Shanghai in the local market is inferior to the Guangzhou and Shenzhen markets, and the attractiveness of the local customer base still needs to be improved.

Exhibit 10: 5-Star Hotels' Seat Turnover Per Day Comparison, by Restaurant Type, Tier 1 Cities, 2022

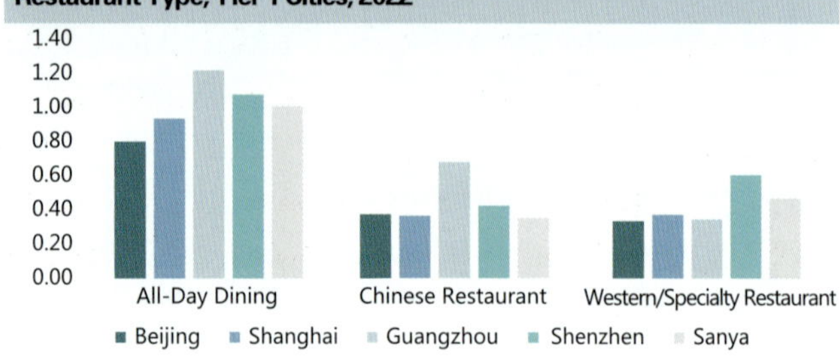

但是，酒店餐饮人并未坐以待毙，这一点在日趋收缩的餐饮开支中可见一斑。2022年，各定位层级酒店市场的每间可供房餐饮开支均呈现一定程度的收紧。五星级酒店的餐饮开支中，尤以人工成本下降幅度最为明显。

即便如此，疫情对于会议宴会和商务宴请这类酒店餐饮最为依仗的客源需求的打击仍是致命的：无法预测的临时封闭限制客人到店用餐；疫情期间，人们也倾向于减少密切往来，而酒店餐厅与社会餐厅相比又多了外地住店客人这一层潜在的接触风险。所以，2022年各定位层级酒店市场每间可供房餐饮利润持续走低，三星及有限服务酒店的利润空间几近为零。

图9：2013年至2022年各定位层级酒店市场每间可供房餐饮利润

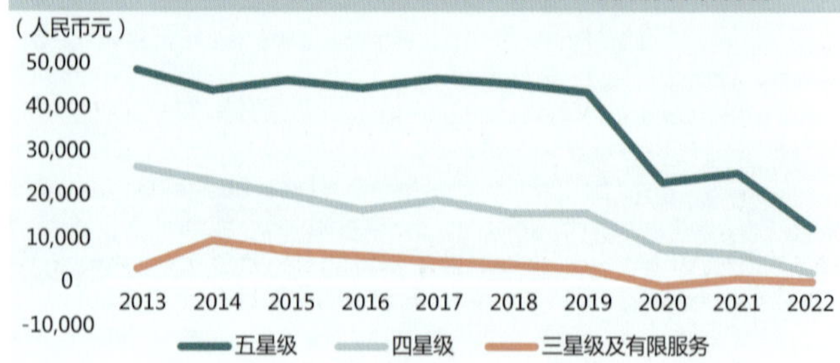

酒店餐饮花式破圈，但“强者恒强”现象始终存在

尽管酒店餐饮面临全面的大幅下跌，但“强者恒强”的道理依旧适用。从核心城市来看，广、深在全日餐厅和中餐厅两个板块仍牢牢霸榜前两名的地位。得益于得天独厚的美食文化，广、深两地居民对于美食的追求和支付意愿都相对更高。酒店餐饮为了在竞争激烈的社会餐饮中博得一席之地花样频出，不仅在菜式和出品上严谨钻研，价格和营销也更接地气，多年来市场中涌现了一批备受当地市民青睐的酒店餐厅。所以，即便受到疫情打击，本地老饕仍为部分酒店餐饮的底气。相较而言，北京和上海两地各餐厅的上座率表现则不如人意：一方面，2022年长达数月的封控严重拉低了餐位的使用率；另一方面，北京和上海的酒店餐饮在本地市场的拓展相对逊色于广、深市场，对于本地客群的吸引力仍有待提升。

图10：2022年各一线市场五星级酒店餐饮设施每日每餐位上座数比较

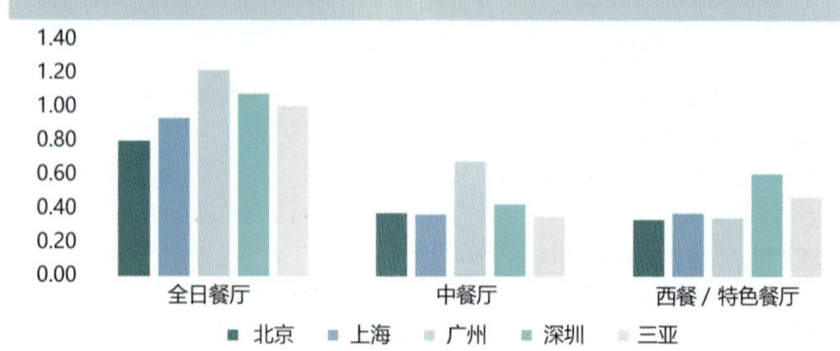

In terms of F&B revenue, the top 20 five-star hotels in first-tier cities and the top 50 in second-tier cities both have F&B revenues and GOPPAR that are much higher than the respective market averages. These results highlight the premium performances of the leading F&B businesses. These hotels not only excelled in the culinary industry, but they also achieved notable strides in the retail industry. The outbreak had a significant impact on room sales, and many hotels changed their business plans to concentrate on local market. As a result, the hotel F&B retail industry developed into a crucial tool for drawing in local customers.

从城市层级来看，纵观一线城市餐饮收入前20名和二线城市前50名的五星级酒店，其每间可供房均摊餐饮收入及利润均远超各自层级市场均值，餐饮领头羊的业绩溢价能力尽显。除了在餐厅板块的优秀表现外，我们发现这些酒店普遍在零售板块也颇有建树。在疫情期间，酒店客房销售遭遇严峻挑战，众多酒店调整策略加码本地生活实现创收，酒店餐饮的零售板块便成为吸引本地客群的重要抓手。

Exhibit 11: F&B Revenue PAR and F&B GOP PAR Comparison, Top 20 5-Star and All 5-Star Hotels, Tier 1 Cities, 2022

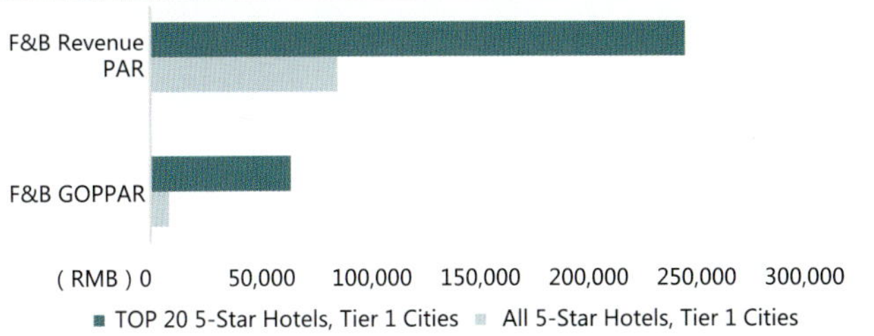

图11：一线城市餐饮收入前20名的五星级酒店每间可供房餐饮收入及利润与一线城市五星级酒店均值比较

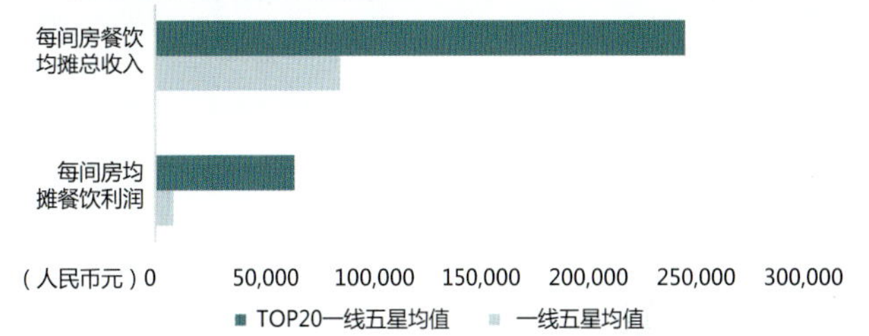

Exhibit 12: F&B Revenue PAR and F&B GOP PAR Comparison, Top 50 5-Star and All 5-Star Hotels, Tier 2 Cities, 2022

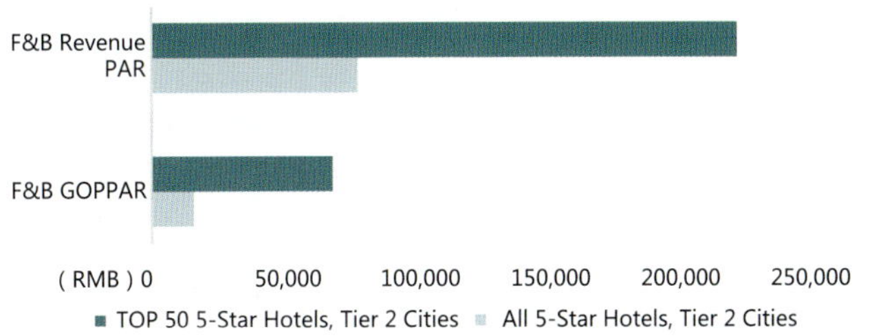

图12：二线城市餐饮收入前50名的五星级酒店每间可供房餐饮收入及利润与二线城市五星级酒店均值比较

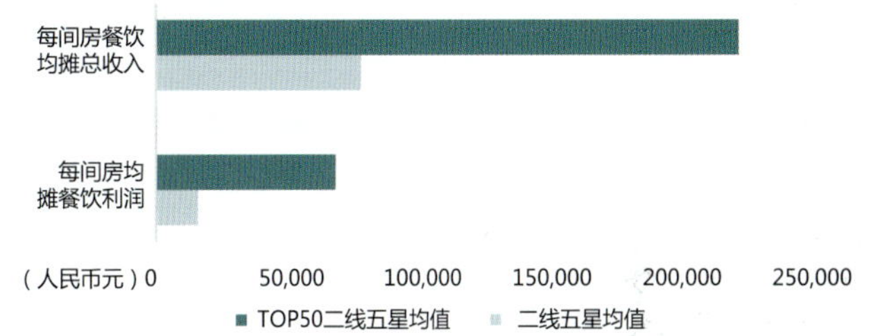

On the one hand, hotels cooperated with online platforms to provide takeaway services and sell pre-made dishes at the entrance of residential areas during lockdowns, targeting local customers and increasing offline traffic. Hotels, on the other hand, also prioritized traditional festivals such as the Mid-Autumn Festival, Dragon Boat Festival, and Spring Festival, and optimized their holiday gift boxes. In addition to high-end products made with expensive ingredients, five-star hotels also offered more affordable and popular options in their holiday gift boxes, including sauce products, food and oil sets, and dry goods. For instance, mooncakes and zongzi no longer merely chase unique flavors; their development also includes classic flavors in order to cater to the taste of the wider public. Hotel F&B had to "break through" during the pandemic lockdown, and retail became a "lifesaver" for certain hotel F&B businesses.

一方面，酒店通过与线上平台合作打通外卖服务，在疫情封控期间在小区门口摆摊出售预制菜品，面向本地客群，带动线下流量的发展。另一方面，酒店对于中秋、端午和春节三个传统节日更为重视全面优化节日礼盒。除了原本有着昂贵食材的高大上产品外，五星级酒店也在放下身段，走接地气的亲民路线：年货礼盒的内容中，酱货、粮油套装、干粮等百花齐放；月饼、粽子也不再一味追求猎奇的口味，而是在传统风味的基础上适度创新，迎合大众口味。疫情封控时代倒逼酒店餐饮"破圈"，餐饮零售也因此成为部分酒店餐饮板块的"救命稻草"。

However, for most hotels, the compensatory benefits provided by "creative self-rescue" are still modest. Using F&B retail as an example, revenue distribution for five-star hotels still follows a traditional pyramid form. Only 1% of hotels achieved over 10 million yuan retail revenue, and these hotels are all "frequent winners" in the F&B sector. Over half of all hotels had F&B retail revenue of less than 1 million yuan. Meanwhile, F&B retail revenue also presents typical regional characteristics: people in the south prefer to buy food during the Dragon Boat Festival and Qingming Festival, while people in the north tend to buy goods for the Chinese New Year.

当然，对于大多数酒店而言，"花式自救"所产生的补偿性收益仍是杯水车薪。以餐饮零售为例，五星级酒店的餐饮零售收入分布呈现典型的金字塔形态。仅有1%的酒店实现了1,000万元以上的零售收入，而这些酒店无一例外均为餐饮的"常胜将军"；餐饮零售收入不足100万元的酒店超过半数。同时，餐饮零售收入也呈现出典型的地域性特征：南方喜过端午和清明，北方人则偏爱买年货。

Exhibit 13: F&B Retail Revenue Distribution, 5 Star Hotels, 2022

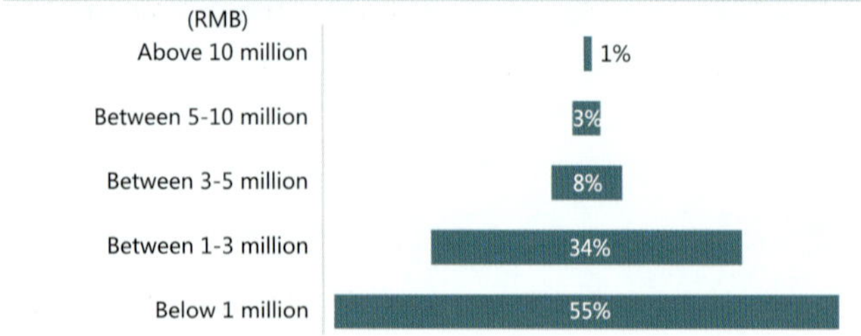

These data clearly suggest that hotel F&B and the F&B retail industry that grew during the pandemic remain selective businesses. Hotels with natural advantages can focus on perfecting individual items. They can make their restaurants stand out from the traditional hotel system, become an additional profit point for hotels and compete on an equal footing with the social catering industry to gain greater visibility on the local market. Conversely, hotels that feel burdened by F&B operations need to rationalize and simplify F&B facilities, put more effort and resources into areas that provide better profits, or seek assistance from external third parties to jointly support the growth of hotel F&B.

Given its limited profitability, the hotel F&B revolution has been ongoing for a long time. Prior to the pandemic, we could already see five-star hotels offer afternoon tea sets, hiring well-known chefs, and developing various seasonal menus. The outbreak accelerated hotel F&B innovation and reform. Hotel practitioners experimented with product iteration and optimizing operational procedures, connecting catering with the local community. Hotel F&B thus entered an era of community in which it is no longer simply dependent on hotel guests. As an integral part of the hotel business, F&B should not only assist hotel operations through multi-scenario and all-time operations, but also strive to build a more market-oriented and socialized hotel catering better adapted to changes in consumer demand. By strengthening its local qualities and implementing new marketing approaches, hotel F&B may become more accessible to local inhabitants and no longer remain a high-end consumption venue that they avoid.

Conclusion

Looking back on the three years of pandemic, the hotel industry has struggled to move forward in a volatile market environment. Unlike the confusion of 2020 and the joy of performance rebound in 2021, the long-term lockdowns in 2022 has prompted hoteliers to consider new product directions in the face of changing consumer patterns, cost control under the heavy revenue pressure, and the industry's future in the face of rapid technological development.

In 2022, the pandemic raged on, severely affecting both tourism and business travel. Although high-end tourist sources remained trapped domestically, the unpredictable lockdowns significantly reduced popular willingness to travel, and the advantage of destination vacation markets was not yet apparent. However, by offering various city exploration activities, high-end local leisure and business hotels became a new favorite and emphasized the importance of excellent product quality. Only products that are market-oriented and meet customer needs possessed the "evergreen charm that passed

图13：2022年五星级酒店餐饮零售收入分布

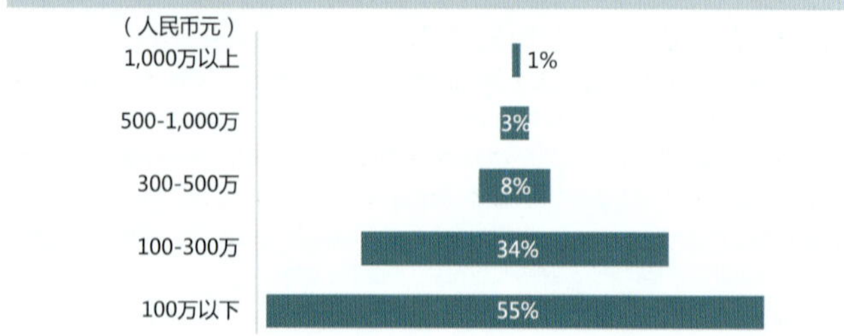

从这些数据中不难看出，酒店餐饮以及疫情期间放大的餐饮零售仍是一门具有选择性的生意：有天然优势的酒店可有的放矢地将单品做到极致，使餐厅从酒店传统体系中脱颖而出，既成为酒店的额外赢利点，也能够与社会餐饮站在同一起跑线上竞争，在本地市场收获更多喝彩。而对于餐饮运营备感负担的酒店则应合理精简餐饮设施，将精力和资源投至收益更高的板块，或寻求外部第三方的协助，共同扶持酒店餐饮的成长。

苦于有限的盈利能力，酒店餐饮的革命由来已久。在疫情前，我们便能看到五星级酒店打造联名下午茶、聘请知名大厨、开发各类季节性菜单。疫情则成为酒店餐饮创新改革的加速器，酒店从业者努力探索产品的迭代和经营方式的优化，打通餐饮与本地的链接，酒店餐饮顺势进入了不再单纯依附于酒店住客的社区化时代。餐饮作为酒店的一部分，未来，除了以多场景、全时段的运营辅助酒店经营外，也应致力于构建更适应市场消费变化的社会化酒店餐饮，增强属地特质，辅以新模式营销，让其不再是本地居民望而却步的高消场所。

总结

回望疫情三年，酒店业在跌宕起伏的市场环境下艰难前行。不同于2020年的迷茫和2021年业绩回调的喜悦，2022年的长时间封控带给了酒店人更多思考，思考消费模式变化下的新产品方向、收入重压下的强本节用、科技快速发展下行业的未来……

2022年疫情肆虐，旅游和商务需求均遭遇沉重打击。尽管高端旅游客源仍被困于国内，但是不可预测的管控大幅降低了人们出行的意愿，目的地度假市场优势不显。而城中的高端休闲商务酒店凭借各类城中探索活动成为新宠，重掀宅度假的风潮，这也再一次印证了优秀产品力的重要性：具备市场前瞻性、契合客群需求的产品方可坐拥穿越黑暗周期的长青魅力。在越发成熟的体验型消费市场，如何深耕细分领域，打造不可复制的产品

through this dark cycle". In an increasingly mature and experiential consumer market, the question of how to cultivate and refine one's practices in segmented fields, or how to create unique product and service labels is one that every practitioner should seriously consider and explore. At the same time, the obstacles and opportunities faced by various sectors during the pandemic, such as F&B and human resources, should be afforded greater attention and placed on the agenda so that they may be handled more efficiently in the future.

As the year goes on, new issues arise. The fact that many countries, including China, have eased pandemic restrictions and a number of demands have formally entered the fast lane of recovery at the time of this study's publication. After three years of dormancy, the hotel sector has now officially started spring. Practitioners should maintain the resilience and determination they showed throughout the pandemic to creatively self-rescue for survival when the current cycle gets underway. They should push forward, actively look for a route that is actually fit for their own growth, defy expectations, and innovate. Additionally, we think that after this pandemic, the hotel sector in China will restart its course of high-quality development, designing novel spaces with more demand-oriented product supply, more scientific and rational operational concepts, and more innovative ideas for development.

The crisis and opportunities brought about by the pandemic are destined to be the touchstone for the future development of the hotel industry. We believe that the road ahead is long but bright! The data in the table below fully demonstrates the rich information provided in this statistical publication. We sincerely thank all industry participants for their continued and strong support of this publication!

Total Respondent Hotels	1,570
Total Participating Hotels (Valid Surveys)	1,505
Total Guest Rooms	434,145
Total Revenue	RMB 71.47 billion
Total Room Revenue	RMB 38.69 billion
Total F&B Revenue	RMB 27.13 billion
Total Staff	317,150
Total F&B Seats	555,689
Total F&B Covers	150 million
City Covered	214
Province Covered	31

Note: To ensure the comparability and continuity of the data, hotels that were closed for a long time due to the pandemic were excluded from the valid surveys.

和服务标签是值得每一位从业者深思和探索的问题。同时，餐饮、人力等诸多板块在疫情期间显露出的难处和机遇也应得到重视，亟待提上妥善处理的日程。

岁将更始，时乃日新。值得欣喜的是，截至本刊物出版之际，包括中国在内的大部分国家已经解除防疫限制，各类需求复苏正式迈入快车道，蛰伏了三年的酒店行业也终于迎来了春天。站在新周期的起点上，从业者更应怀揣着疫情期间为了生存“花式自救”的勇气和决心，砥砺前行，在仍旧充满了诸多不确定性的后疫情时期，积极探索真正适合自身发展的道路，打破陈规，开拓创新。我们相信，经此一疫，中国酒店行业将重新踏上高质量发展的道路，以更为贴合需求的产品供给、更加科学理性的运营理念、更具革新精神的发展思路，开辟全新的想象空间。

疫情带来的危与机注定是酒店行业未来发展的试金石，我们相信，前路漫漫亦灿灿！下表数据充分展现了这本统计刊物涵盖的丰富信息量，我们真诚感谢所有行业参与者对本刊物的持续大力支持！

回复问卷酒店总数	1,570家
有效问卷酒店总数	1,505家
客房总数	434,145间
总营业收入	714.7亿元
客房总收入	386.9亿元
餐饮总收入	271.3亿元
员工总数	317,150名
餐饮总餐位数	555,689个
餐饮总上座人数	1.5亿人次
涵盖城市总数	214个
涵盖省份	31个

备注：为确保数据的可对标性和连续性，在有效问卷的筛选中剔除了受疫情影响长时间停业的酒店。

表 1 酒店业业务摘要（2022 / 2021）

2022	以星级分类 By Star Rating			以管理模式分类 By Management Model				以城市等级分类 By City Category			
	五星 5-Star	四星 4-Star	三星+有限服务 3-Star + Limited Service	国际管理 International 五星/5-Star	国内管理 Domestic 五星/5-Star	国际管理 International 四星/4-Star	国内管理 Domestic 四星/4-Star	一线城市 Tier 1 cities 五星/5-Star	二线城市 Tier 2 cities 五星/5-Star	三线城市 Tier 3 cities 五星/5-Star	目的地度假村 Destination Resort 五星/5-Star
业务摘要											
酒店数量(家)	976	367	162	673	290	189	165	201	477	141	157
每日可供出租客房数(间)	311,373	92,189	30,583	214,733	92,578	51,221	38,773	70,699	155,960	41,663	43,052
每日实际入住客房数(间)	133,321	41,496	15,486	94,314	37,604	23,152	17,269	28,823	71,382	16,827	16,272
平均住宿率	42.8%	45.0%	50.6%	43.9%	40.6%	45.2%	44.5%	40.8%	45.8%	40.4%	37.8%
平均房价(元)	649	398	324	730	468	431	357	804	573	410	994
每间可供出租客房收入(元)	278	179	164	321	190	195	159	328	262	165	376
每间可供出租客房总收入(元)	189,503	113,066	76,390	207,117	149,401	109,658	115,231	230,528	183,892	126,917	203,157
每间可供出租客房总支出(元)	165,224	102,027	56,161	177,642	52,143	97,970	103,229	213,310	156,712	120,111	160,479
每间可供出租房经营毛利(元)	**24,771**	**11,155**	**20,587**	**29,693**	**15,367**	**12,135**	**10,238**	**17,895**	**27,592**	**6,938**	**42,867**
经营毛利率	13.1%	9.9%	27.0%	14.3%	10.3%	11.1%	8.9%	7.8%	15.0%	5.5%	21.1%
管理费(基本及奖金)(元)	5,530	3,227	2,684	5,855	4,045	2,971	3,092	5,908	5,488	3,290	7,163
非经营相关收入及支出前收益(元)	**19,883**	**8,421**	**18,271**	**23,967**	**12,673**	**8,922**	**8,535**	**12,559**	**22,877**	**3,955**	**36,236**

2021	以星级分类 By Star Rating			以管理模式分类 By Management Model				以城市等级分类 By City Category			
	五星 5-Star	四星 4-Star	三星+有限服务 3-Star + Limited Service	国际管理 International 五星/5-Star	国内管理 Domestic 五星/5-Star	国际管理 International 四星/4-Star	国内管理 Domestic 四星/4-Star	一线城市 Tier 1 cities 五星/5-Star	二线城市 Tier 2 cities 五星/5-Star	三线城市 Tier 3 cities 五星/5-Star	目的地度假村 Destination Resort 五星/5-Star
业务摘要											
酒店数量(家)	975	343	217	633	342	182	161	216	469	172	118
每日可供出租客房数(间)	312,067	85,467	37,211	204,734	107,333	48,357	37,110	76,116	152,210	49,717	34,025
每日实际入住客房数(间)	153,562	41,656	19,975	104,593	48,996	24,362	17,283	40,393	75,361	22,750	14,975
平均住宿率	49.2%	48.7%	53.7%	51.1%	45.6%	50.4%	46.6%	53.1%	49.5%	45.8%	44.0%
平均房价(元)	693	419	314	778	513	441	387	845	615	435	1,069
每间可供出租客房收入(元)	341	204	168	397	234	222	180	448	304	199	470
每间可供出租客房总收入(元)	233,576	129,621	82,013	259,617	183,927	126,911	133,152	319,391	214,162	153,417	244,849
每间可供出租客房总支出(元)	181,310	113,033	56,751	197,725	149,807	107,170	120,840	246,974	167,677	131,359	166,978
每间可供出租房经营毛利(元)	**53,944**	**18,945**	**27,205**	**63,157**	**36,265**	**19,741**	**18,245**	**72,696**	**49,064**	**22,517**	**79,311**
经营毛利率	23.1%	14.6%	33.2%	24.3%	19.7%	15.6%	13.7%	22.8%	22.9%	14.7%	32.4%
管理费(基本及奖金)(元)	8,087	3,614	3,037	8,733	7,163	3,714	3,241	10,527	7,196	4,460	11,648
非经营相关收入及支出前收益(元)	**46,186**	**15,950**	**23,906**	**54,341**	**30,639**	**16,051**	**15,816**	**62,245**	**42,216**	**18,450**	**68,781**

备注 Notes:

1. 国际管理：由国际饭店管理公司管理或者挂牌的酒店。
   Int'l: operated and managed by an international Hotel Management Company (HMC) or franchised by an international HMC.
2. 国内管理：由国内饭店管理公司管理或者挂牌的酒店。
   Dom.: operated and managed by a domestic Hotel Management Company (HMC) or franchised by a domestic HMC.
3. GOP: Gross Operating Profit

TABLE 1　INDUSTRY SUMMARY（2022 VS. 2021）

2022	以平均房价分类 By Average Room Rate				以主要市场分类 By Key Market				
	¥ 1,000 以上 Above ¥ 1,000	¥ 701~1,000 Between ¥ 701-1,000	¥ 401~700 Between ¥ 401-700	¥ 400 及以下 Below ¥ 400	北京 Beijing 五星/5-Star	上海 Shanghai 五星/5-Star	广州 Guangzhou 五星/5-Star	深圳 Shenzhen 五星/5-Star	三亚 Sanya 五星/5-Star
Industry Summary									
Number of Hotels	159	169	618	559	68	79	34	29	28
Number of Available Rooms per Day	41,931	52,743	195,109	144,362	23,915	27,685	12,776	9,168	10,277
Number of Occupied Rooms per Day	16,502	22,256	86,340	65,130	7,779	11,808	6,332	3,971	4,721
Occupancy	39.4%	42.2%	44.3%	45.1%	32.5%	42.7%	49.6%	43.3%	45.9%
Average Room Rate (RMB)	1,468	809	522	325	922	781	749	875	1,353
Revenue Per Available Room - RevPAR (RMB)	578	341	231	147	300	333	371	379	621
Total Revenue Per Available Room (RMB)	364,634	230,736	154,853	98,217	201,243	215,547	304,244	266,087	302,749
Total Expenses Per Available Room (RMB)	287,710	199,646	139,604	89,118	202,657	201,862	248,902	235,784	209,288
GOP Per Available Room (RMB)	**76,923**	**31,972**	**15,640**	**9,555**	**(1,413)**	**16,356**	**53,553**	**30,304**	**93,461**
As % of Total Revenue	21.1%	13.9%	10.1%	9.7%	(0.7%)	7.6%	17.6%	11.4%	30.9%
Management Fees (Base + Incentive) (RMB)	12,180	6,234	4,230	2,669	4,585	5,348	8,716	7,375	11,383
Income Before Non-operating Income and Expenses (RMB)	**64,903**	**26,358**	**11,859**	**7,485**	**(5,231)**	**11,196**	**45,752**	**23,329**	**82,078**

2021	以平均房价分类 By Average Room Rate				以主要市场分类 By Key Market				
	¥ 1,000 以上 Above ¥ 1,000	¥ 701~1,000 Between ¥ 701-1,000	¥ 401~700 Between ¥ 401-700	¥ 400 及以下 Below ¥ 400	北京 Beijing 五星/5-Star	上海 Shanghai 五星/5-Star	广州 Guangzhou 五星/5-Star	深圳 Shenzhen 五星/5-Star	三亚 Sanya 五星/5-Star
Industry Summary									
Number of Hotels	160	184	641	550	73	76	35	32	32
Number of Available Rooms per Day	41,679	59,450	202,700	130,915	25,889	27,103	12,836	10,288	11,313
Number of Occupied Rooms per Day	22,553	30,488	100,525	61,523	12,489	15,321	6,829	5,761	6,926
Occupancy	54.1%	51.3%	49.6%	47.0%	48.2%	56.5%	53.2%	56.0%	61.2%
Average Room Rate (RMB)	1,455	815	528	319	831	840	783	958	1,312
Revenue Per Available Room - RevPAR (RMB)	787	418	262	150	401	475	417	537	803
Total Revenue Per Available Room (RMB)	493,606	280,808	180,355	100,840	284,161	316,794	349,924	376,792	408,900
Total Expenses Per Available Room (RMB)	337,435	213,113	148,134	88,232	227,397	241,103	274,603	277,187	247,854
GOP Per Available Room (RMB)	**160,246**	**67,695**	**32,582**	**15,795**	**56,764**	**76,456**	**75,321**	**99,605**	**161,046**
As % of Total Revenue	32.5%	24.1%	18.1%	15.7%	20.0%	24.1%	21.5%	26.4%	39.4%
Management Fees (Base + Incentive) (RMB)	20,347	9,875	5,379	2,988	9,233	10,128	11,778	13,295	19,692
Income Before Non-operating Income and Expenses (RMB)	**140,658**	**58,233**	**27,727**	**13,115**	**48,563**	**66,567**	**60,823**	**87,066**	**143,095**

备注 Notes:

1. 一线城市包括北京、上海、广州和深圳。
   Tier 1 cities include Beijing, Shanghai, Guangzhou and Shenzhen.
2. 二线城市包括省会城市和省内经济都会城市，例如苏州、厦门等。
   Tier 2 cities refer to provincial capital cities and provincial economic centre cities such as Suzhou and Xiamen.
3. 三线城市包括除一线、二线城市及知名旅游目的地外的城市，例如保定、洛阳、遵义等。
   Tier 3 cities include cities other than Tier 1 and Tier 2 cities and well-known tourist destinations, such as Baoding, Luoyang, Zunyi, etc.
4. 旅游目的地包括中国知名旅游目的地，例如三亚、丽江、千岛湖等。
   Tourism destinations refer to renowned vacation destinations like Sanya, Lijiang and Qiandao Lake.

表 2　部门收支

	以星级分类 By Star Rating			以管理模式分类 By Management Model				以城市等级分类 By City Category			
	五星 5-Star	四星 4-Star	三星+有限服务 3-Star + Limited Service	国际管理 International 五星/5-Star	国内管理 Domestic 五星/5-Star	国际管理 International 四星/4-Star	国内管理 Domestic 四星/4-Star	一线城市 Tier 1 cities 五星/5-Star	二线城市 Tier 2 cities 五星/5-Star	三线城市 Tier 3 cities 五星/5-Star	目的地度假村 Destination Resort 五星/5-Star
部门收支											
以每间可供出租客房计算	（元）	（元）	（元）	（元）	（元）	（元）	（元）	（元）	（元）	（元）	（元）
部门收入											
客房	100,819	64,880	57,152	115,336	68,331	70,556	57,438	117,983	94,707	59,149	135,716
食品	57,171	29,548	13,846	59,311	52,366	26,457	33,037	61,112	60,059	50,535	46,486
饮品	2,678	881	413	2,924	2,114	564	1,317	4,464	2,373	1,453	1,983
其他餐饮	15,943	8,209	3,237	17,668	11,286	7,635	9,319	21,546	16,953	9,873	8,874
水疗及健身	4,133	2,618	1,776	4,034	4,424	1,888	4,860	5,583	3,378	2,717	5,200
其他营运部门	4,389	7,983	5,947	2,711	7,902	2,014	15,238	7,179	3,649	3,676	3,356
杂项收入	5,662	4,398	3,632	5,635	5,628	3,093	5,747	9,923	4,625	3,184	4,641
合计	**189,503**	**113,066**	**76,390**	**207,117**	**149,401**	**109,658**	**115,231**	**230,528**	**183,892**	**126,917**	**203,157**
部门支出											
客房	29,290	19,798	14,000	32,729	21,175	19,809	18,962	38,083	27,018	18,625	33,356
餐饮	62,768	34,693	14,729	66,420	54,006	31,589	38,318	78,198	63,047	49,751	48,951
水疗及健身	3,329	2,038	1,467	3,438	2,892	1,483	3,891	3,769	2,327	2,082	6,600
其他营运部门	3,755	5,800	4,540	2,322	6,583	1,647	8,302	4,158	3,313	4,326	4,188
合计	**98,029**	**58,153**	**30,557**	**104,116**	**82,527**	**53,457**	**61,226**	**123,549**	**94,918**	**73,169**	**91,431**
部门盈利(亏损)											
客房	71,530	45,082	43,151	82,607	47,156	50,746	38,475	79,900	67,689	40,524	102,360
餐饮	13,024	3,945	2,768	13,482	11,759	3,068	5,355	8,924	16,339	12,109	8,392
水疗及健身	804	579	309	596	1,532	404	969	1,814	1,050	636	(1,399)
其他营运部门	634	2,183	1,407	389	1,319	367	6,936	3,021	337	(650)	(832)
杂项收入	5,662	4,398	3,632	5,635	5,628	3,093	5,747	9,923	4,625	3,184	4,641
合计	**91,473**	**54,913**	**45,833**	**103,002**	**66,874**	**56,201**	**54,005**	**106,979**	**88,974**	**53,747**	**111,726**
未分配经营开支											
行政及一般开支	23,387	17,215	10,570	24,108	21,242	15,759	18,301	32,448	21,338	16,972	22,225
信息及通信系统	4,736	3,039	1,353	5,329	1,595	3,288	1,227	6,444	4,311	3,068	4,384
市场推广及营销	11,400	6,258	4,150	13,259	7,250	6,939	5,130	15,404	10,731	7,110	11,298
能源	17,315	10,811	6,821	18,571	14,316	11,312	10,234	20,573	16,487	13,831	18,255
物业营运及保养	11,410	7,722	4,129	12,453	8,896	7,386	7,912	16,046	9,624	7,615	13,951
合计	**67,194**	**43,874**	**25,604**	**73,526**	**52,143**	**44,513**	**42,003**	**89,761**	**61,793**	**46,942**	**69,048**
经营毛利	**24,771**	**11,155**	**20,587**	**29,693**	**15,367**	**12,135**	**10,238**	**17,895**	**27,592**	**6,938**	**42,867**
管理费(基本及奖金)	5,530	3,227	2,684	5,855	4,045	2,971	3,092	5,908	5,488	3,290	7,163
非经营相关收入及支出前收益	**19,883**	**8,421**	**18,271**	**23,967**	**12,673**	**8,922**	**8,535**	**12,559**	**22,877**	**3,955**	**36,236**

备注 Note:

1. 类项与往年主要差别为取消通信部门及租金收入，增添杂项收入以及信息及通信系统部门。这一变更的依据是第十一版《酒店业统一会计制度》。
   The coloms were updated according to the eleventh revised edition of Uniform System of Accounts for the Lodging Industry. The key changes are canceling telecommunications department and rental & other income, and adding miscellaneous income and information & telecommunications department.
2. 纵向合计将不会完全符合，所有平均数据只平均为该行提供数据的酒店。
   Vertical totals will not always add up since averages were only based on hotels that contributed data to the specific line item.

TABLE 2 DEPARTMENTAL REVENUES & EXPENSES

	以平均房价分类 By Average Room Rate				以主要市场分类 By Key Market				
	¥ 1,000 以上 Above ¥ 1,000	¥ 701~1,000 Between ¥ 701-1,000	¥ 401~700 Between ¥ 401-700	¥ 400 及以下 Below ¥ 400	北京 Beijing 五星/5-Star	上海 Shanghai 五星/5-Star	广州 Guangzhou 五星/5-Star	深圳 Shenzhen 五星/5-Star	三亚 Sanya 五星/5-Star
Dept. Rev. & Exp.									
Per Available Room	**RMB**	**RMB**	**RMB**	**RMB**	**RMB**	**RMB**	**RMB**	**RMB**	**RMB**
Departmental Revenues									
Rooms	209,299	124,094	83,324	52,221	108,862	118,835	133,605	138,336	226,766
Food	94,649	66,233	45,769	32,687	37,260	57,445	95,947	85,516	54,187
Beverage	8,768	3,460	1,240	1,006	2,751	3,640	8,085	5,449	3,348
Other Food & Beverage	27,510	18,731	14,097	6,875	16,785	18,047	34,725	25,231	8,016
Spa & Fitness Center	8,581	4,581	2,974	2,311	7,981	4,072	5,794	4,789	3,938
Other Operated Depts.	5,540	4,348	5,091	5,579	9,899	3,793	11,349	3,315	2,164
Miscellaneous Income	11,088	7,035	4,772	3,200	11,384	8,493	12,066	6,778	5,303
Total	**364,634**	**230,736**	**154,853**	**98,217**	**201,243**	**215,547**	**304,244**	**266,087**	**302,749**
Departmental Expenses									
Rooms	54,748	36,584	24,942	15,910	35,906	37,527	42,438	42,846	49,525
Food & Beverage	106,058	74,971	51,705	33,537	62,010	73,560	105,989	95,537	57,339
Spa & Fitness Center	8,149	3,388	2,103	1,784	4,378	3,567	3,894	4,095	9,136
Other Operated Depts.	4,137	3,484	3,662	5,368	4,897	3,503	5,187	3,305	2,858
Total	**172,193**	**117,631**	**81,189**	**52,918**	**107,111**	**117,213**	**156,737**	**144,211**	**118,179**
Departmental Profit (Loss)									
Rooms	154,551	87,510	58,381	36,311	72,956	81,308	91,166	95,490	177,241
Food & Beverage	24,869	13,453	9,402	7,031	(5,214)	5,571	32,767	20,659	8,210
Spa & Fitness Center	432	1,193	871	528	3,603	504	1,900	693	(5,198)
Other Operated Depts.	1,403	864	1,429	211	5,002	291	6,162	10	(694)
Miscellaneous Income	11,088	7,035	4,772	3,200	11,384	8,493	12,066	6,778	5,303
Total	**192,440**	**113,105**	**73,664**	**45,299**	**94,132**	**98,334**	**147,507**	**121,876**	**184,570**
Undistributed Operating Expenses									
Administrative & General	38,019	28,315	21,056	13,922	36,971	28,892	32,925	30,564	27,175
Information & Telecommunications	7,758	5,615	4,047	2,109	5,998	6,078	5,901	6,489	5,442
Marketing	21,976	14,569	9,310	5,263	14,269	15,770	15,780	16,904	16,010
Energy	27,378	20,039	15,001	10,230	21,523	19,288	22,232	21,829	23,284
Property Operation & Maintenance	20,961	14,081	9,680	6,152	18,939	14,851	16,784	13,894	19,759
Total	**115,517**	**82,015**	**58,415**	**36,200**	**95,545**	**84,649**	**92,165**	**91,573**	**91,109**
Gross Operating Profit	**76,923**	**31,972**	**15,640**	**9,555**	**(1,413)**	**16,356**	**53,553**	**30,304**	**93,461**
Management Fees (Base + Incentive)	12,180	6,234	4,230	2,669	4,585	5,348	8,716	7,375	11,383
Income Before Non-operating Income and Expenses	**64,903**	**26,358**	**11,859**	**7,485**	**(5,231)**	**11,196**	**45,752**	**23,329**	**82,078**

表 2 部门收支（续1）

	以星级分类 By Star Rating			以管理模式分类 By Management Model				以城市等级分类 By City Category			
	五星 5-Star	四星 4-Star	三星+有限服务 3-Star + Limited Service	国际管理 International 五星/5-Star	国内管理 Domestic 五星/5-Star	国际管理 International 四星/4-Star	国内管理 Domestic 四星/4-Star	一线城市 Tier 1 cities 五星/5-Star	二线城市 Tier 2 cities 五星/5-Star	三线城市 Tier 3 cities 五星/5-Star	目的地度假村 Destination Resort 五星/5-Star
部门收支											
以每间实际入住客房计算	（元）	（元）	（元）	（元）	（元）	（元）	（元）	（元）	（元）	（元）	（元）
部门收入											
客房	655	399	331	731	469	434	356	804	574	410	1,008
食品	371	183	85	376	356	163	207	416	364	347	342
饮品	17	5	3	19	14	3	8	30	14	10	15
其他餐饮	103	51	20	112	77	47	60	147	103	68	65
水疗及健身	27	17	12	26	30	12	35	36	21	20	37
其他营运部门	28	49	38	17	53	12	95	49	22	25	25
杂项收入	36	28	23	35	38	19	38	67	28	22	34
合计	**1,230**	**698**	**439**	**1,311**	**1,022**	**676**	**718**	**1,570**	**1,115**	**879**	**1,494**
部门支出											
客房	190	122	83	207	145	122	118	259	164	129	245
餐饮	407	214	87	421	369	195	239	532	382	345	360
水疗及健身	22	13	9	22	20	9	30	25	14	15	47
其他营运部门	24	36	28	15	45	10	53	28	20	29	31
合计	**636**	**359**	**178**	**659**	**564**	**330**	**381**	**841**	**576**	**507**	**672**
部门盈利(亏损)											
客房	465	277	248	524	324	311	238	544	410	281	763
餐饮	84	25	21	85	79	19	37	61	99	80	62
水疗及健身	5	4	2	4	11	3	5	12	6	5	(10)
其他营运部门	4	13	10	2	8	2	42	21	2	(4)	(7)
杂项收入	36	28	23	35	38	19	38	67	28	22	34
合计	**594**	**339**	**261**	**652**	**457**	**346**	**336**	**729**	**540**	**372**	**822**
未分配经营开支											
行政及一般开支	152	106	63	153	145	97	114	221	129	117	163
信息及通信系统	30	19	8	34	11	20	7	43	26	20	32
市场推广及营销	74	39	25	84	50	43	32	105	65	49	83
能源	112	67	40	118	98	70	64	140	100	95	135
物业营运及保养	74	48	24	79	61	46	49	109	58	53	103
合计	**435**	**271**	**153**	**466**	**355**	**275**	**262**	**611**	**375**	**322**	**508**
经营毛利	**161**	**69**	**121**	**188**	**105**	**75**	**64**	**122**	**167**	**48**	**315**
管理费(基本及奖金)	36	20	16	37	28	18	20	40	33	22	52
非经营相关收入及支出前收益	**129**	**52**	**107**	**152**	**86**	**55**	**54**	**85**	**139**	**27**	**266**

备注 Note:

1. 纵向合计将不会完全符合，所有平均数据只平均为该行提供数据的酒店。
   Vertical totals will not always add up since averages were only based on hotels that contributed data to the specific line item.

TABLE 2 DEPARTMENTAL REVENUES & EXPENSES（CONT.）

	以平均房价分类 By Average Room Rate				以主要市场分类 By Key Market				
	¥ 1,000 以上 Above ¥ 1,000	¥ 701~1,000 Between ¥ 701-1,000	¥ 401~700 Between ¥ 401-700	¥ 400 及以下 Below ¥400	北京 Beijing 五星/5-Star	上海 Shanghai 五星/5-Star	广州 Guangzhou 五星/5-Star	深圳 Shenzhen 五星/5-Star	三亚 Sanya 五星/5-Star
Dept. Rev. & Exp.									
Per Occupied Room	**RMB**	**RMB**	**RMB**	**RMB**	**RMB**	**RMB**	**RMB**	**RMB**	**RMB**
Departmental Revenues									
Rooms	1,469	817	524	325	922	781	749	875	1,353
Food	664	437	288	206	316	378	538	541	323
Beverage	62	23	8	6	24	24	45	34	20
Other Food & Beverage	193	124	89	44	144	119	195	161	48
Spa & Fitness Center	59	30	19	15	67	25	30	30	24
Other Operated Depts.	39	29	32	35	85	25	62	21	13
Miscellaneous Income	77	46	30	20	98	56	64	43	32
Total	**2,560**	**1,522**	**974**	**611**	**1,705**	**1,417**	**1,705**	**1,683**	**1,806**
Departmental Expenses									
Rooms	384	241	157	100	304	247	237	271	295
Food & Beverage	744	494	326	210	525	484	592	604	342
Spa & Fitness Center	56	22	13	11	37	23	20	26	55
Other Operated Depts.	29	23	23	34	43	23	29	21	17
Total	**1,209**	**776**	**511**	**330**	**908**	**770**	**876**	**912**	**705**
Departmental Profit (Loss)									
Rooms	1,085	576	367	226	618	534	512	604	1,057
Food & Beverage	175	89	59	46	(42)	36	185	131	49
Spa & Fitness Center	3	8	5	4	30	3	10	4	(31)
Other Operated Depts.	10	6	9	1	42	2	33	1	(4)
Miscellaneous Income	77	46	30	20	98	56	64	43	32
Total	**1,351**	**746**	**463**	**281**	**798**	**646**	**829**	**771**	**1,101**
Undistributed Operating Expenses									
Administrative & General	267	187	133	87	314	189	184	193	162
Information & Telecommunications	54	36	25	13	50	39	32	40	32
Marketing	154	96	59	33	121	104	88	107	95
Energy	192	132	94	64	182	127	124	138	139
Property Operation & Maintenance	147	93	61	38	160	98	93	88	118
Total	**811**	**541**	**368**	**226**	**810**	**555**	**515**	**579**	**543**
Gross Operating Profit	**540**	**211**	**98**	**60**	**(12)**	**107**	**299**	**192**	**557**
Management Fees (Base + Incentive)	86	40	27	17	38	35	47	47	68
Income Before Non-operating Income and Expenses	**456**	**174**	**75**	**47**	**(44)**	**73**	**256**	**148**	**490**

表 2 部门收支（续2）

	以星级分类 By Star Rating			以管理模式分类 By Management Model				以城市等级分类 By City Category			
	五星 5-Star	四星 4-Star	三星+有限服务 3-Star + Limited Service	国际管理 International 五星/5-Star	国内管理 Domestic 五星/5-Star	国际管理 International 四星/4-Star	国内管理 Domestic 四星/4-Star	一线城市 Tier 1 cities 五星/5-Star	二线城市 Tier 2 cities 五星/5-Star	三线城市 Tier 3 cities 五星/5-Star	目的地度假村 Destination Resort 五星/5-Star
部门收支											
以百分比计算											
部门收入											
客房	53%	57%	75%	56%	46%	64%	50%	51%	52%	47%	67%
食品	30%	26%	18%	29%	35%	24%	29%	27%	33%	40%	23%
饮品	1%	1%	1%	1%	1%	1%	1%	2%	1%	1%	1%
其他餐饮	8%	7%	4%	9%	8%	7%	8%	9%	9%	8%	4%
水疗及健身	2%	2%	2%	2%	3%	2%	4%	2%	2%	2%	3%
其他营运部门	2%	7%	8%	1%	5%	2%	13%	3%	2%	3%	2%
杂项收入	3%	4%	5%	3%	4%	3%	5%	4%	3%	3%	2%
合计	**100%**	**100%**	**100%**	**100%**	**100%**	**100%**	**100%**	**100%**	**100%**	**100%**	**100%**
部门支出											
客房	29%	31%	24%	28%	31%	28%	33%	32%	29%	31%	25%
餐饮	83%	93%	96%	83%	83%	92%	95%	90%	80%	82%	86%
水疗及健身	81%	78%	83%	85%	65%	79%	80%	68%	69%	77%	127%
其他营运部门	86%	73%	76%	86%	83%	82%	54%	58%	91%	118%	125%
合计	**52%**	**51%**	**40%**	**50%**	**55%**	**49%**	**53%**	**54%**	**52%**	**58%**	**45%**
部门盈利(亏损)											
客房	71%	69%	76%	72%	69%	72%	67%	68%	71%	69%	75%
餐饮	17%	7%	4%	17%	17%	8%	5%	10%	20%	18%	14%
水疗及健身	19%	22%	17%	15%	35%	21%	20%	32%	31%	23%	(27%)
其他营运部门	14%	27%	24%	14%	17%	18%	46%	42%	9%	(18%)	(25%)
杂项收入	100%	100%	100%	100%	100%	100%	100%	100%	100%	100%	100%
合计	**48%**	**49%**	**60%**	**50%**	**45%**	**51%**	**47%**	**46%**	**48%**	**42%**	**55%**
未分配经营开支											
行政及一般开支	12%	15%	14%	12%	14%	14%	16%	14%	12%	13%	11%
信息及通信系统	2%	3%	2%	3%	1%	3%	1%	3%	2%	2%	2%
市场推广及营销	6%	6%	5%	6%	5%	6%	4%	7%	6%	6%	6%
能源	9%	10%	9%	9%	10%	10%	9%	9%	9%	11%	9%
物业营运及保养	6%	7%	5%	6%	6%	7%	7%	7%	5%	6%	7%
合计	**35%**	**39%**	**34%**	**35%**	**35%**	**41%**	**36%**	**39%**	**34%**	**37%**	**34%**
经营毛利	**13%**	**10%**	**27%**	**14%**	**10%**	**11%**	**9%**	**8%**	**15%**	**5%**	**21%**
管理费(基本及奖金)	3%	3%	4%	3%	3%	3%	3%	3%	3%	3%	4%
非经营相关收入及支出前收益	**10%**	**7%**	**24%**	**12%**	**8%**	**8%**	**7%**	**5%**	**12%**	**3%**	**18%**

备注 Note:

1. 纵向合计将不会完全符合，所有平均数据只平均为该行提供数据的酒店。
   Vertical totals will not always add up since averages were only based on hotels that contributed data to the specific line item.
2. 各部门支出百分比以其部门收入为基础，其他未分配部门以总收入为基础。
   Expense ratios for departmental expenses are based on their respective departmental revenues, all other expenses are based on total revenue.

	以平均房价分类 By Average Room Rate				以主要市场分类 By Key Market				
	¥ 1,000 以上 Above ¥ 1,000	¥ 701~1,000 Between ¥ 701-1,000	¥ 401~700 Between ¥ 401-700	¥ 400 及以下 Below ¥400	北京 Beijing 五星/5-Star	上海 Shanghai 五星/5-Star	广州 Guangzhou 五星/5-Star	深圳 Shenzhen 五星/5-Star	三亚 Sanya 五星/5-Star
Dept. Rev. & Exp.									
% of Revenue									
Departmental Revenues									
Rooms	57%	54%	54%	53%	54%	55%	44%	52%	75%
Food	26%	29%	30%	33%	19%	27%	32%	32%	18%
Beverage	2%	1%	1%	1%	1%	2%	3%	2%	1%
Other Food & Beverage	8%	8%	9%	7%	8%	8%	11%	9%	3%
Spa & Fitness Center	2%	2%	2%	2%	4%	2%	2%	2%	1%
Other Operated Depts.	2%	2%	3%	6%	5%	2%	4%	1%	1%
Miscellaneous Income	3%	3%	3%	3%	6%	4%	4%	3%	2%
Total	**100%**	**100%**	**100%**	**100%**	**100%**	**100%**	**100%**	**100%**	**100%**
Departmental Expenses									
Rooms	26%	29%	30%	30%	33%	32%	32%	31%	22%
Food & Beverage	81%	85%	85%	86%	110%	93%	76%	83%	87%
Spa & Fitness Center	95%	74%	71%	77%	55%	88%	67%	86%	232%
Other Operated Depts.	75%	80%	72%	96%	49%	92%	46%	100%	132%
Total	**47%**	**51%**	**52%**	**54%**	**53%**	**54%**	**52%**	**54%**	**39%**
Departmental Profit (Loss)									
Rooms	74%	71%	70%	70%	67%	68%	68%	69%	78%
Food & Beverage	19%	15%	15%	14%	(10%)	7%	24%	17%	13%
Spa & Fitness Center	5%	26%	29%	23%	45%	12%	33%	14%	(132%)
Other Operated Depts.	25%	20%	28%	4%	51%	8%	54%	0%	(32%)
Miscellaneous Income	100%	100%	100%	100%	100%	100%	100%	100%	100%
Total	**53%**	**49%**	**48%**	**46%**	**47%**	**46%**	**48%**	**46%**	**61%**
Undistributed Operating Expenses									
Administrative & General	10%	12%	14%	14%	18%	13%	11%	11%	9%
Information & Telecommunications	2%	2%	3%	2%	3%	3%	2%	2%	2%
Marketing	6%	6%	6%	5%	7%	7%	5%	6%	5%
Energy	8%	9%	10%	10%	11%	9%	7%	8%	8%
Property Operation & Maintenance	6%	6%	6%	6%	9%	7%	6%	5%	7%
Total	**32%**	**36%**	**38%**	**37%**	**47%**	**39%**	**30%**	**34%**	**30%**
Gross Operating Profit	**21%**	**14%**	**10%**	**10%**	**(1%)**	**8%**	**18%**	**11%**	**31%**
Management Fees (Base + Incentive)	3%	3%	3%	3%	2%	2%	3%	3%	4%
Income Before Non-operating Income and Expenses	**18%**	**11%**	**8%**	**8%**	**(3%)**	**5%**	**15%**	**9%**	**27%**

表 3　客房部门

	以星级分类 By Star Rating			以管理模式分类 By Management Model				以城市等级分类 By City Category			
	五星 5-Star	四星 4-Star	三星+有限服务 3-Star + Limited Service	国际管理 International 五星/5-Star	国内管理 Domestic 五星/5-Star	国际管理 International 四星/4-Star	国内管理 Domestic 四星/4-Star	一线城市 Tier 1 cities 五星/5-Star	二线城市 Tier 2 cities 五星/5-Star	三线城市 Tier 3 cities 五星/5-Star	目的地度假村 Destination Resort 五星/5-Star
部门收支											
以每间可供出租客房计算	（元）	（元）	（元）	（元）	（元）	（元）	（元）	（元）	（元）	（元）	（元）
客房收入	**100,819**	**64,880**	**57,152**	**115,336**	**68,331**	**70,556**	**57,438**	**117,983**	**94,707**	**59,149**	**135,716**
工资及相关开支	15,183	11,160	9,458	16,485	12,047	10,980	11,255	19,563	14,196	10,613	15,964
其他开支	14,113	8,565	5,147	16,200	9,184	8,865	8,057	18,318	12,872	8,121	17,392
客房部门开支合计	**29,290**	**19,798**	**14,000**	**32,729**	**21,175**	**19,809**	**18,962**	**38,083**	**27,018**	**18,625**	**33,356**
客房部门盈利(亏损)	**71,530**	**45,082**	**43,151**	**82,607**	**47,156**	**50,746**	**38,475**	**79,900**	**67,689**	**40,524**	**102,360**
以每间实际入住客房计算											
客房收入	**655**	**399**	**331**	**731**	**469**	**434**	**356**	**804**	**574**	**410**	**1,008**
工资及相关开支	99	69	57	104	82	68	70	133	86	73	117
其他开支	92	53	31	103	63	55	50	125	78	56	128
客房部门开支合计	**190**	**122**	**83**	**207**	**145**	**122**	**118**	**259**	**164**	**129**	**245**
客房部门盈利(亏损)	**465**	**277**	**248**	**524**	**324**	**311**	**238**	**544**	**410**	**281**	**763**
以占部门收入百分比计算											
客房收入	**100.0%**	**100.0%**	**100.0%**	**100.0%**	**100.0%**	**100.0%**	**100.0%**	**100.0%**	**100.0%**	**100.0%**	**100.0%**
工资及相关开支	15.1%	17.2%	16.5%	14.3%	17.6%	15.6%	19.6%	16.6%	15.0%	17.9%	11.8%
其他开支	14.0%	13.2%	9.0%	14.0%	13.4%	12.6%	14.0%	15.5%	13.6%	13.7%	12.8%
客房部门开支合计	**29.1%**	**30.5%**	**24.5%**	**28.4%**	**31.0%**	**28.1%**	**33.0%**	**32.3%**	**28.5%**	**31.5%**	**24.6%**
客房部门盈利(亏损)	**70.9%**	**69.5%**	**75.5%**	**71.6%**	**69.0%**	**71.9%**	**67.0%**	**67.7%**	**71.5%**	**68.5%**	**75.4%**

备注 Notes:

1. 纵向合计将不会完全符合，所有平均数据只平均为该行提供数据的酒店。
   Vertical totals will not always add up since averages were only based on hotels that contributed data to the specific line item.

TABLE 3 ROOMS DEPARTMENT

	以平均房价分类 By Average Room Rate				以主要市场分类 By Key Market				
	¥ 1,000 以上 Above ¥ 1,000	¥ 701~1,000 Between ¥ 701-1,000	¥ 401~700 Between ¥ 401-700	¥ 400 及以下 Below ¥400	北京 Beijing 五星/5-Star	上海 Shanghai 五星/5-Star	广州 Guangzhou 五星/5-Star	深圳 Shenzhen 五星/5-Star	三亚 Sanya 五星/5-Star
Rooms Department									
Per Available Room	**RMB**	**RMB**	**RMB**	**RMB**	**RMB**	**RMB**	**RMB**	**RMB**	**RMB**
Rooms Revenue	**209,299**	**124,094**	**83,324**	**52,221**	**108,862**	**118,835**	**133,605**	**138,336**	**226,766**
Payroll & Related Expenses	25,787	18,616	13,424	9,472	20,060	19,229	19,811	20,249	20,307
All Other Expenses	28,617	18,068	11,616	6,465	15,846	17,781	22,628	22,597	29,218
Total Rooms Expenses	**54,748**	**36,584**	**24,942**	**15,910**	**35,906**	**37,527**	**42,438**	**42,846**	**49,525**
Rooms Department Profit (Loss)	**154,551**	**87,510**	**58,381**	**36,311**	**72,956**	**81,308**	**91,166**	**95,490**	**177,241**
Per Occupied Room									
Rooms Revenue	**1,469**	**817**	**524**	**325**	**922**	**781**	**749**	**875**	**1,353**
Payroll & Related Expenses	181	123	84	59	170	126	111	128	121
All Other Expenses	201	120	73	41	134	117	126	143	174
Total Rooms Expenses	**384**	**241**	**157**	**100**	**304**	**247**	**237**	**271**	**295**
Rooms Department Profit (Loss)	**1,085**	**576**	**367**	**226**	**618**	**534**	**512**	**604**	**1,057**
% of Departmental Revenue									
Rooms Revenue	**100.0%**	**100.0%**	**100.0%**	**100.0%**	**100.0%**	**100.0%**	**100.0%**	**100.0%**	**100.0%**
Payroll & Related Expenses	12.3%	15.0%	16.1%	18.1%	18.4%	16.2%	14.8%	14.6%	9.0%
All Other Expenses	13.7%	14.6%	13.9%	12.4%	14.6%	15.0%	16.9%	16.3%	12.9%
Total Rooms Expenses	**26.2%**	**29.5%**	**29.9%**	**30.5%**	**33.0%**	**31.6%**	**31.8%**	**31.0%**	**21.8%**
Rooms Department Profit (Loss)	**73.8%**	**70.5%**	**70.1%**	**69.5%**	**67.0%**	**68.4%**	**68.2%**	**69.0%**	**78.2%**

	以星级分类 By Star Rating			以管理模式分类 By Management Model				以城市等级分类 By City Category			
	五星 5-Star	四星 4-Star	三星+有限服务 3-Star + Limited Service	国际管理 International 五星/5-Star	国内管理 Domestic 五星/5-Star	国际管理 International 四星/4-Star	国内管理 Domestic 四星/4-Star	一线城市 Tier 1 cities 五星/5-Star	二线城市 Tier 2 cities 五星/5-Star	三线城市 Tier 3 cities 五星/5-Star	目的地度假村 Destination Resort 五星/5-Star
餐饮部门											
以每间可供出租客房计算	（元）	（元）	（元）	（元）	（元）	（元）	（元）	（元）	（元）	（元）	（元）
食品收入	57,171	29,548	13,846	59,311	52,366	26,457	33,037	61,112	60,059	50,535	46,486
饮品收入	2,678	881	413	2,924	2,114	564	1,317	4,464	2,373	1,453	1,983
其他收入	15,943	8,209	3,237	17,668	11,286	7,635	9,319	21,546	16,953	9,873	8,874
总餐饮收入	**75,308**	**37,261**	**15,333**	**79,792**	**64,742**	**34,415**	**40,423**	**86,839**	**78,899**	**60,859**	**57,167**
食品直接成本	24,213	13,783	6,905	24,369	23,736	11,590	15,963	24,975	25,864	22,740	18,358
饮品直接成本	997	424	218	879	1,077	295	587	1,270	996	935	605
餐饮直接成本合计	**25,196**	**14,173**	**7,066**	**25,246**	**24,767**	**11,877**	**16,471**	**26,233**	**26,843**	**23,670**	**18,954**
工资及相关开支	29,186	16,070	6,452	31,871	22,879	15,354	17,127	40,231	27,564	20,607	25,137
其他开支	8,313	4,940	2,334	8,997	6,688	4,414	5,656	11,002	8,672	5,836	4,904
工资及其他开支合计	**37,499**	**21,010**	**8,785**	**40,869**	**29,567**	**19,768**	**22,783**	**51,233**	**36,236**	**26,443**	**30,041**
餐饮部门开支合计	**62,768**	**34,693**	**14,729**	**66,420**	**54,006**	**31,589**	**38,318**	**78,198**	**63,047**	**49,751**	**48,951**
餐饮部门盈利(亏损)	**12,540**	**2,568**	**605**	**13,371**	**10,736**	**2,827**	**2,105**	**8,641**	**15,853**	**11,108**	**8,216**
以每间实际入住客房计算											
食品收入	371	183	85	376	356	163	207	416	364	347	342
饮品收入	17	5	3	19	14	3	8	30	14	10	15
其他收入	103	51	20	112	77	47	60	147	103	68	65
总餐饮收入	**489**	**230**	**93**	**505**	**443**	**212**	**252**	**591**	**479**	**422**	**420**
食品直接成本	157	85	40	154	162	72	100	170	157	157	135
饮品直接成本	6	3	1	6	7	2	4	9	6	6	4
餐饮直接成本合计	**163**	**88**	**42**	**160**	**169**	**73**	**103**	**179**	**163**	**164**	**139**
工资及相关开支	189	99	38	202	156	95	107	274	167	143	185
其他开支	54	31	14	57	46	27	36	75	53	40	36
工资及其他开支合计	**243**	**130**	**52**	**259**	**202**	**122**	**142**	**349**	**220**	**183**	**221**
餐饮部门开支合计	**407**	**214**	**87**	**421**	**369**	**195**	**239**	**532**	**382**	**345**	**360**
餐饮部门盈利(亏损)	**82**	**16**	**6**	**85**	**74**	**17**	**13**	**59**	**96**	**78**	**60**
以占部门收入百分比计算											
食品收入	75.4%	76.5%	79.1%	74.2%	79.6%	76.3%	75.6%	70.1%	75.7%	81.7%	81.1%
饮品收入	3.5%	2.3%	2.4%	3.7%	3.2%	1.6%	3.0%	5.1%	3.0%	2.3%	3.5%
其他收入	21.0%	21.2%	18.5%	22.1%	17.2%	22.0%	21.3%	24.7%	21.4%	16.0%	15.5%
总餐饮收入	**100.0%**	**100.0%**	**100.0%**	**100.0%**	**100.0%**	**100.0%**	**100.0%**	**100.0%**	**100.0%**	**100.0%**	**100.0%**
食品直接成本	42.4%	46.6%	49.9%	41.1%	45.3%	43.8%	48.3%	40.9%	43.1%	45.0%	39.5%
饮品直接成本	37.2%	48.1%	52.8%	30.1%	50.9%	52.3%	44.6%	28.4%	42.0%	64.3%	30.5%
餐饮直接成本合计	**42.1%**	**46.6%**	**49.6%**	**40.6%**	**45.5%**	**44.0%**	**47.9%**	**40.0%**	**43.0%**	**45.5%**	**39.1%**
工资及相关开支	38.8%	43.1%	42.1%	39.9%	35.3%	44.6%	42.4%	46.3%	34.9%	33.9%	44.0%
其他开支	11.0%	13.3%	15.2%	11.3%	10.3%	12.8%	14.0%	12.7%	11.0%	9.6%	8.6%
工资及其他开支合计	**49.8%**	**56.4%**	**57.3%**	**51.2%**	**45.7%**	**57.4%**	**56.4%**	**59.0%**	**45.9%**	**43.4%**	**52.5%**
餐饮部门开支合计	**83.3%**	**93.1%**	**96.1%**	**83.2%**	**83.4%**	**91.8%**	**94.8%**	**90.0%**	**79.9%**	**81.7%**	**85.6%**
餐饮部门盈利(亏损)	**16.7%**	**6.9%**	**3.9%**	**16.8%**	**16.6%**	**8.2%**	**5.2%**	**10.0%**	**20.1%**	**18.3%**	**14.4%**

备注 Notes:

1. 纵向合计将不会完全符合，所有平均数据只平均为该行提供数据的酒店。
Vertical totals will not always add up since averages were only based on hotels that contributed data to the specific line item.

TABLE 4 FOOD & BEVERAGE DEPARTMENT

	以平均房价分类 By Average Room Rate				以主要市场分类 By Key Market				
	¥ 1,000 以上 Above ¥ 1,000	¥ 701~1,000 Between ¥ 701-1,000	¥ 401~700 Between ¥ 401-700	¥ 400 及以下 Below ¥ 400	北京 Beijing 五星/5-Star	上海 Shanghai 五星/5-Star	广州 Guangzhou 五星/5-Star	深圳 Shenzhen 五星/5-Star	三亚 Sanya 五星/5-Star
Food & Beverage Department									
Per Available Room	**RMB**	**RMB**	**RMB**	**RMB**	**RMB**	**RMB**	**RMB**	**RMB**	**RMB**
Food Revenue	94,649	66,233	45,769	32,687	37,260	57,445	95,947	85,516	54,187
Beverage Revenue	8,768	3,460	1,240	1,006	2,751	3,640	8,085	5,449	3,348
Other Revenue	27,510	18,731	14,097	6,875	16,785	18,047	34,725	25,231	8,016
Total F&B Revenue	**130,739**	**88,120**	**60,487**	**38,837**	**56,504**	**79,035**	**138,756**	**115,228**	**65,550**
Food Cost	35,545	27,633	20,323	14,965	15,581	22,372	41,094	35,672	19,130
Beverage Cost	2,674	893	616	584	699	851	2,729	1,761	817
Total Cost of Goods Sold	**38,188**	**28,517**	**20,938**	**15,479**	**16,270**	**23,214**	**43,823**	**37,432**	**19,947**
Payroll & Related Expenses	52,924	36,264	23,621	14,486	38,073	38,722	44,596	44,713	32,089
All Other Expenses	13,325	10,334	7,366	4,150	8,314	9,170	17,570	13,392	5,304
Total Payroll & Related Expenses	**66,249**	**46,598**	**30,986**	**18,635**	**46,387**	**47,892**	**62,166**	**58,105**	**37,393**
Total F&B Expenses	**106,058**	**74,971**	**51,705**	**33,537**	**62,010**	**73,560**	**105,989**	**95,537**	**57,339**
F&B Department Profit (Loss)	**24,681**	**13,149**	**8,783**	**5,301**	**(5,506)**	**5,475**	**32,767**	**19,690**	**8,210**
Per Occupied Room									
Food Revenue	664	437	288	206	316	378	538	541	323
Beverage Revenue	62	23	8	6	24	24	45	34	20
Other Revenue	193	124	89	44	144	119	195	161	48
Total F&B Revenue	**918**	**581**	**381**	**244**	**479**	**520**	**778**	**728**	**391**
Food Cost	250	182	128	94	132	147	230	226	114
Beverage Cost	19	6	4	4	6	6	15	11	5
Total Cost of Goods Sold	**268**	**188**	**132**	**97**	**138**	**153**	**245**	**237**	**119**
Payroll & Related Expenses	372	239	149	90	324	255	249	283	191
All Other Expenses	94	68	46	26	70	60	98	85	32
Total Payroll & Related Expenses	**465**	**308**	**195**	**117**	**394**	**315**	**347**	**367**	**223**
Total F&B Expenses	**744**	**494**	**326**	**210**	**525**	**484**	**592**	**604**	**342**
F&B Department Profit (Loss)	**173**	**87**	**55**	**34**	**(47)**	**36**	**185**	**124**	**49**
% of Departmental Revenue									
Food Revenue	72.3%	74.9%	74.9%	80.6%	65.6%	72.6%	69.1%	73.6%	82.7%
Beverage Revenue	6.7%	3.9%	2.0%	2.5%	4.8%	4.6%	5.8%	4.7%	5.1%
Other Revenue	21.0%	21.2%	23.1%	16.9%	29.6%	22.8%	25.0%	21.7%	12.2%
Total F&B Revenue	**100.0%**	**100.0%**	**100.0%**	**100.0%**	**100.0%**	**100.0%**	**100.0%**	**100.0%**	**100.0%**
Food Cost	37.6%	41.7%	44.4%	45.8%	41.8%	38.9%	42.8%	41.7%	35.3%
Beverage Cost	30.5%	25.8%	49.6%	58.1%	25.4%	23.4%	33.8%	32.3%	24.4%
Total Cost of Goods Sold	**36.9%**	**40.9%**	**44.5%**	**45.9%**	**40.7%**	**38.0%**	**42.1%**	**41.2%**	**34.7%**
Payroll & Related Expenses	40.5%	41.2%	39.1%	37.3%	67.4%	49.0%	32.1%	38.8%	49.0%
All Other Expenses	10.2%	11.7%	12.2%	10.7%	14.7%	11.6%	12.7%	11.6%	8.1%
Total Payroll & Related Expenses	**50.7%**	**52.9%**	**51.2%**	**48.0%**	**82.1%**	**60.6%**	**44.8%**	**50.4%**	**57.0%**
Total F&B Expenses	**81.1%**	**85.1%**	**85.5%**	**86.4%**	**109.7%**	**93.1%**	**76.4%**	**82.9%**	**87.5%**
F&B Department Profit (Loss)	**18.9%**	**14.9%**	**14.5%**	**13.6%**	**(9.7%)**	**6.9%**	**23.6%**	**17.1%**	**12.5%**

表 5　水疗 / 健身部门及其他营运部门

	以星级分类 By Star Rating			以管理模式分类 By Management Model				以城市等级分类 By City Category			
	五星 5-Star	四星 4-Star	三星+有限服务 3-Star + Limited Service	国际管理 International 五星/5-Star	国内管理 Domestic 五星/5-Star	国际管理 International 四星/4-Star	国内管理 Domestic 四星/4-Star	一线城市 Tier 1 cities 五星/5-Star	二线城市 Tier 2 cities 五星/5-Star	三线城市 Tier 3 cities 五星/5-Star	目的地度假村 Destination Resort 五星/5-Star
SPA及健身部门											
以每间可供出租客房计算	（元）	（元）	（元）	（元）	（元）	（元）	（元）	（元）	（元）	（元）	（元）
部门收入	**4,133**	**2,618**	**1,776**	**4,034**	**4,424**	**1,888**	**4,860**	**5,583**	**3,378**	**2,717**	**5,200**
直接成本	340	644	108	254	541	129	1,989	500	177	482	511
工资及相关开支	2,484	1,451	1,396	2,586	2,156	1,218	2,078	2,978	1,828	1,355	4,428
其他开支	780	313	244	803	714	324	273	780	481	450	1,967
部门开支合计	**3,329**	**2,038**	**1,467**	**3,438**	**2,892**	**1,483**	**3,891**	**3,769**	**2,327**	**2,082**	**6,600**
部门盈利(亏损)	**804**	**579**	**309**	**596**	**1,532**	**404**	**969**	**1,814**	**1,050**	**636**	**(1,399)**
以每间实际入住客房计算											
部门收入	**27**	**17**	**12**	**26**	**30**	**12**	**35**	**36**	**21**	**20**	**37**
直接成本	2	4	1	2	4	1	16	3	1	3	4
工资及相关开支	16	9	9	16	15	8	16	19	11	10	32
其他开支	5	2	2	5	5	2	2	5	3	3	14
部门开支合计	**22**	**13**	**9**	**22**	**20**	**9**	**30**	**25**	**14**	**15**	**47**
部门盈利(亏损)	**5**	**4**	**2**	**4**	**11**	**3**	**5**	**12**	**6**	**5**	**(10)**
以占部门收入百分比计算											
部门收入	**100.0%**	**100.0%**	**100.0%**	**100.0%**	**100.0%**	**100.0%**	**100.0%**	**100.0%**	**100.0%**	**100.0%**	**100.0%**
直接成本	8.2%	24.6%	6.1%	6.3%	12.2%	6.8%	40.9%	8.9%	5.2%	17.7%	9.8%
工资及相关开支	60.1%	55.4%	78.6%	64.1%	48.7%	64.6%	42.8%	53.3%	54.1%	49.9%	85.2%
其他开支	18.9%	12.0%	13.8%	19.9%	16.1%	17.2%	5.6%	14.0%	14.2%	16.6%	37.8%
部门开支合计	**80.5%**	**77.9%**	**82.6%**	**85.2%**	**65.4%**	**78.6%**	**80.1%**	**67.5%**	**68.9%**	**76.6%**	**126.9%**
部门盈利(亏损)	**19.5%**	**22.1%**	**17.4%**	**14.8%**	**34.6%**	**21.4%**	**19.9%**	**32.5%**	**31.1%**	**23.4%**	**(26.9%)**
其他营运部门											
以每间可供出租客房计算	（元）	（元）	（元）	（元）	（元）	（元）	（元）	（元）	（元）	（元）	（元）
部门收入	**4,389**	**7,983**	**5,947**	**2,711**	**7,902**	**2,014**	**15,238**	**7,179**	**3,649**	**3,676**	**3,356**
直接成本	1,355	2,782	1,692	972	2,226	654	3,418	1,124	1,171	2,188	1,740
工资及相关开支	2,509	3,285	3,424	1,851	3,724	1,418	5,664	3,228	2,150	2,409	2,727
其他开支	823	2,478	3,830	142	2,080	108	2,943	1,026	818	815	503
部门开支合计	**3,755**	**5,800**	**4,540**	**2,322**	**6,583**	**1,647**	**8,302**	**4,158**	**3,313**	**4,326**	**4,188**
部门盈利(亏损)	**634**	**2,183**	**1,407**	**389**	**1,319**	**367**	**6,936**	**3,021**	**337**	**(650)**	**(832)**
以每间实际入住客房计算											
部门收入	**28**	**49**	**38**	**17**	**53**	**12**	**95**	**49**	**22**	**25**	**25**
直接成本	9	17	10	6	15	4	21	8	7	14	13
工资及相关开支	16	20	20	12	26	9	36	22	13	16	20
其他开支	5	15	26	1	14	1	19	7	5	5	4
部门开支合计	**24**	**36**	**28**	**15**	**45**	**10**	**53**	**28**	**20**	**29**	**31**
部门盈利(亏损)	**4**	**13**	**10**	**2**	**8**	**2**	**42**	**21**	**2**	**(4)**	**(7)**
以占部门收入百分比计算											
部门收入	**100.0%**	**100.0%**	**100.0%**	**100.0%**	**100.0%**	**100.0%**	**100.0%**	**100.0%**	**100.0%**	**100.0%**	**100.0%**
直接成本	30.9%	34.8%	28.5%	35.9%	28.2%	32.5%	22.4%	15.7%	32.1%	59.5%	51.8%
工资及相关开支	57.2%	41.1%	57.6%	68.3%	47.1%	70.4%	37.2%	45.0%	58.9%	65.5%	81.3%
其他开支	18.8%	31.0%	64.4%	5.2%	26.3%	5.4%	19.3%	14.3%	22.4%	22.2%	15.0%
部门开支合计	**85.6%**	**72.7%**	**76.3%**	**85.6%**	**83.3%**	**81.8%**	**54.5%**	**57.9%**	**90.8%**	**117.7%**	**124.8%**
部门盈利(亏损)	**14.4%**	**27.3%**	**23.7%**	**14.4%**	**16.7%**	**18.2%**	**45.5%**	**42.1%**	**9.2%**	**(17.7%)**	**(24.8%)**

备注 Notes:

1. 纵向合计将不会完全符合，所有平均数据只平均为该行提供数据的酒店。
   Vertical totals will not always add up since averages were only based on hotels that contributed data to the specific line item.

	以平均房价分类 By Average Room Rate				以主要市场分类 By Key Market				
	¥ 1,000 以上 Above ¥ 1,000	¥ 701~1,000 Between ¥ 701-1,000	¥ 401~700 Between ¥ 401-700	¥ 400 及以下 Below ¥400	北京 Beijing 五星/5-Star	上海 Shanghai 五星/5-Star	广州 Guangzhou 五星/5-Star	深圳 Shenzhen 五星/5-Star	三亚 Sanya 五星/5-Star
SPA & Fitness Center									
Per Available Room	**RMB**	**RMB**	**RMB**	**RMB**	**RMB**	**RMB**	**RMB**	**RMB**	**RMB**
Departmental Revenue	**8,581**	**4,581**	**2,974**	**2,311**	**7,981**	**4,072**	**5,794**	**4,789**	**3,938**
Cost of Sales	640	300	236	547	977	244	366	254	530
Payroll & Related Expenses	5,621	2,685	1,641	1,243	3,378	2,804	2,940	3,214	6,927
All Other Expenses	2,115	687	463	289	960	745	820	895	1,781
Total Departmental Expenses	**8,149**	**3,388**	**2,103**	**1,784**	**4,378**	**3,567**	**3,894**	**4,095**	**9,136**
Departmental Profit (Loss)	**432**	**1,193**	**871**	**528**	**3,603**	**504**	**1,900**	**693**	**(5,198)**
Per Occupied Room									
Departmental Revenue	**59**	**30**	**19**	**15**	**67**	**25**	**30**	**30**	**24**
Cost of Sales	4	2	1	3	8	2	2	2	3
Payroll & Related Expenses	39	18	10	8	28	18	15	20	42
All Other Expenses	15	4	3	2	8	5	4	6	11
Total Departmental Expenses	**56**	**22**	**13**	**11**	**37**	**23**	**20**	**26**	**55**
Departmental Profit (Loss)	**3**	**8**	**5**	**4**	**30**	**3**	**10**	**4**	**(31)**
% of Departmental Revenue									
Departmental Revenue	**100.0%**	**100.0%**	**100.0%**	**100.0%**	**100.0%**	**100.0%**	**100.0%**	**100.0%**	**100.0%**
Cost of Sales	7.5%	6.6%	7.9%	23.7%	12.2%	6.0%	6.3%	5.3%	13.5%
Payroll & Related Expenses	65.5%	58.6%	55.2%	53.8%	42.3%	68.9%	50.8%	67.1%	175.9%
All Other Expenses	24.6%	15.0%	15.6%	12.5%	12.0%	18.3%	14.2%	18.7%	45.2%
Total Departmental Expenses	**95.0%**	**74.0%**	**70.7%**	**77.2%**	**54.9%**	**87.6%**	**67.2%**	**85.5%**	**232.0%**
Departmental Profit (Loss)	**5.0%**	**26.0%**	**29.3%**	**22.8%**	**45.1%**	**12.4%**	**32.8%**	**14.5%**	**(132.0%)**
Other Operated Departments									
Per Available Room	**RMB**	**RMB**	**RMB**	**RMB**	**RMB**	**RMB**	**RMB**	**RMB**	**RMB**
Departmental Revenue	**5,540**	**4,348**	**5,091**	**5,579**	**9,899**	**3,793**	**11,349**	**3,315**	**2,164**
Cost of Sales	1,447	1,405	1,144	2,627	1,567	825	1,281	739	1,271
Payroll & Related Expenses	3,119	2,892	2,594	2,573	4,281	2,556	3,099	3,771	3,227
All Other Expenses	557	482	891	2,396	733	1,109	1,390	1,041	(1,278)
Total Departmental Expenses	**4,137**	**3,484**	**3,662**	**5,368**	**4,897**	**3,503**	**5,187**	**3,305**	**2,858**
Departmental Profit (Loss)	**1,403**	**864**	**1,429**	**211**	**5,002**	**291**	**6,162**	**10**	**(694)**
Per Occupied Room									
Departmental Revenue	**39**	**29**	**32**	**35**	**85**	**25**	**62**	**21**	**13**
Cost of Sales	10	9	7	16	13	5	7	5	8
Payroll & Related Expenses	22	19	17	16	41	17	18	23	20
All Other Expenses	4	3	6	15	7	7	8	6	(8)
Total Departmental Expenses	**29**	**23**	**23**	**34**	**43**	**23**	**29**	**21**	**17**
Departmental Profit (Loss)	**10**	**6**	**9**	**1**	**42**	**2**	**33**	**1**	**(4)**
% of Departmental Revenue									
Departmental Revenue	**100.0%**	**100.0%**	**100.0%**	**100.0%**	**100.0%**	**100.0%**	**100.0%**	**100.0%**	**100.0%**
Cost of Sales	26.1%	32.3%	22.5%	47.1%	15.8%	21.8%	11.3%	22.3%	58.8%
Payroll & Related Expenses	56.3%	66.5%	51.0%	46.1%	43.2%	67.4%	27.3%	113.8%	149.2%
All Other Expenses	10.1%	11.1%	17.5%	43.0%	7.4%	29.2%	12.3%	31.4%	(59.1%)
Total Departmental Expenses	**74.7%**	**80.1%**	**71.9%**	**96.2%**	**49.5%**	**92.3%**	**45.7%**	**99.7%**	**132.1%**
Departmental Profit (Loss)	**25.3%**	**19.9%**	**28.1%**	**3.8%**	**50.5%**	**7.7%**	**54.3%**	**0.3%**	**(32.1%)**

表 6　未分配经营开支

	以星级分类 By Star Rating			以管理模式分类 By Management Model				以城市等级分类 By City Category			
	五星 5-Star	四星 4-Star	三星+有限服务 3-Star + Limited Service	国际管理 International 五星/5-Star	国内管理 Domestic 五星/5-Star	国际管理 International 四星/4-Star	国内管理 Domestic 四星/4-Star	一线城市 Tier 1 cities 五星/5-Star	二线城市 Tier 2 cities 五星/5-Star	三线城市 Tier 3 cities 五星/5-Star	目的地度假村 Destination Resort 五星/5-Star
行政及一般开支											
以每间可供出租客房计算	（元）	（元）	（元）	（元）	（元）	（元）	（元）	（元）	（元）	（元）	（元）
工资及相关开支	17,638	12,675	7,616	18,134	16,176	11,545	13,922	24,071	16,023	13,424	17,101
其他开支	5,775	4,601	3,516	5,919	5,232	4,250	4,655	8,126	5,393	3,769	5,149
部门开支合计	**23,387**	**17,215**	**10,570**	**24,108**	**21,242**	**15,759**	**18,301**	**32,448**	**21,338**	**16,972**	**22,225**
以每间实际入住客房计算											
工资及相关开支	114	78	46	115	111	71	88	164	97	93	126
其他开支	37	28	22	37	36	26	29	55	33	26	38
部门开支合计	**152**	**106**	**63**	**153**	**145**	**97**	**114**	**221**	**129**	**117**	**163**
以占总收入百分比计算											
工资及相关开支	9.3%	11.2%	10.0%	8.8%	10.8%	10.5%	12.1%	10.4%	8.7%	10.6%	8.4%
其他开支	3.0%	4.1%	4.6%	2.9%	3.5%	3.9%	4.0%	3.5%	2.9%	3.0%	2.5%
部门开支合计	**12.3%**	**15.2%**	**13.8%**	**11.6%**	**14.2%**	**14.4%**	**15.9%**	**14.1%**	**11.6%**	**13.4%**	**10.9%**
信息及通信系统											
以每间可供出租客房计算	（元）	（元）	（元）	（元）	（元）	（元）	（元）	（元）	（元）	（元）	（元）
工资及相关开支	1,275	887	526	1,319	764	823	689	1,545	1,251	787	1,166
其他开支	3,592	2,334	1,296	4,037	1,133	2,546	856	5,056	3,161	2,435	3,377
部门开支合计	**4,736**	**3,039**	**1,353**	**5,329**	**1,595**	**3,288**	**1,227**	**6,444**	**4,311**	**3,068**	**4,384**
以每间实际入住客房计算											
工资及相关开支	8	5	3	8	5	5	4	10	8	5	9
其他开支	23	14	8	25	8	16	5	34	19	16	25
部门开支合计	**30**	**19**	**8**	**34**	**11**	**20**	**7**	**43**	**26**	**20**	**32**
以占总收入百分比计算											
工资及相关开支	0.7%	0.8%	0.7%	0.6%	0.5%	0.8%	0.6%	0.7%	0.7%	0.6%	0.6%
其他开支	1.9%	2.1%	1.7%	1.9%	0.8%	2.3%	0.7%	2.2%	1.7%	1.9%	1.7%
部门开支合计	**2.5%**	**2.7%**	**1.8%**	**2.6%**	**1.1%**	**3.0%**	**1.1%**	**2.8%**	**2.3%**	**2.4%**	**2.2%**

备注 Notes:

1. 纵向合计将不会完全符合，所有平均数据只平均为该行提供数据的酒店。
   Vertical totals will not always add up since averages were only based on hotels that contributed data to the specific line item.

TABLE 6 UNDISTRIBUTED OPERATING EXPENSES

	以平均房价分类 By Average Room Rate				以主要市场分类 By Key Market				
	¥ 1,000 以上 Above ¥ 1,000	¥ 701~1,000 Between ¥ 701-1,000	¥ 401~700 Between ¥ 401-700	¥ 400 及以下 Below ¥ 400	北京 Beijing 五星/5-Star	上海 Shanghai 五星/5-Star	广州 Guangzhou 五星/5-Star	深圳 Shenzhen 五星/5-Star	三亚 Sanya 五星/5-Star
Administration & General									
Per Available Room	**RMB**	**RMB**	**RMB**	**RMB**	**RMB**	**RMB**	**RMB**	**RMB**	**RMB**
Payroll & Related Expenses	28,539	21,543	15,502	10,761	28,793	21,666	22,874	20,734	20,543
All Other Expenses	9,114	6,828	5,663	3,299	8,177	6,615	10,050	9,830	6,632
Total Departmental Expenses	**38,019**	**28,315**	**21,056**	**13,922**	**36,971**	**28,892**	**32,925**	**30,564**	**27,175**
Per Occupied Room									
Payroll & Related Expenses	200	142	98	68	245	142	128	131	123
All Other Expenses	64	45	36	21	70	43	56	62	40
Total Departmental Expenses	**267**	**187**	**133**	**87**	**314**	**189**	**184**	**193**	**162**
% of Total Revenue									
Payroll & Related Expenses	7.8%	9.3%	10.0%	11.0%	14.3%	10.1%	7.5%	7.8%	6.8%
All Other Expenses	2.5%	3.0%	3.7%	3.4%	4.1%	3.1%	3.3%	3.7%	2.2%
Total Departmental Expenses	**10.4%**	**12.3%**	**13.6%**	**14.2%**	**18.4%**	**13.4%**	**10.8%**	**11.5%**	**9.0%**
Information & Telecommunications									
Per Available Room	**RMB**	**RMB**	**RMB**	**RMB**	**RMB**	**RMB**	**RMB**	**RMB**	**RMB**
Payroll & Related Expenses	2,107	1,472	1,034	762	1,594	1,388	1,728	1,640	1,300
All Other Expenses	5,745	4,226	3,136	1,618	4,653	4,740	4,344	5,116	4,181
Total Departmental Expenses	**7,758**	**5,615**	**4,047**	**2,109**	**5,998**	**6,078**	**5,901**	**6,489**	**5,442**
Per Occupied Room									
Payroll & Related Expenses	15	9	6	5	13	9	9	10	8
All Other Expenses	40	27	20	10	39	31	23	32	25
Total Departmental Expenses	**54**	**36**	**25**	**13**	**50**	**39**	**32**	**40**	**32**
% of Total Revenue									
Payroll & Related Expenses	0.6%	0.6%	0.7%	0.8%	0.8%	0.6%	0.6%	0.6%	0.4%
All Other Expenses	1.6%	1.8%	2.0%	1.6%	2.3%	2.2%	1.4%	1.9%	1.4%
Total Departmental Expenses	**2.1%**	**2.4%**	**2.6%**	**2.1%**	**3.0%**	**2.8%**	**1.9%**	**2.4%**	**1.8%**

表 6　未分配经营开支（续）

	以星级分类 By Star Rating			以管理模式分类 By Management Model				以城市等级分类 By City Category			
	五星 5-Star	四星 4-Star	三星+有限服务 3-Star + Limited Service	国际管理 International 五星/5-Star	国内管理 Domestic 五星/5-Star	国际管理 International 四星/4-Star	国内管理 Domestic 四星/4-Star	一线城市 Tier 1 cities 五星/5-Star	二线城市 Tier 2 cities 五星/5-Star	三线城市 Tier 3 cities 五星/5-Star	目的地度假村 Destination Resort 五星/5-Star
市场推广及营销											
以每间可供出租客房计算	（元）	（元）	（元）	（元）	（元）	（元）	（元）	（元）	（元）	（元）	（元）
工资及相关开支	6,245	4,045	2,510	6,948	4,666	4,070	3,941	8,626	5,877	4,084	5,699
品牌系统市场推广费用	2,384	1,121	959	2,458	2,072	1,267	766	2,746	2,236	1,657	2,952
特许加盟费	2,440	1,140	2,932	2,490	2,905	1,312	632	2,430	2,305	371	3,954
其他开支	3,166	1,628	1,026	3,824	1,662	1,784	1,188	4,234	2,933	2,059	3,260
部门开支合计	**11,400**	**6,258**	**4,150**	**13,259**	**7,250**	**6,939**	**5,130**	**15,404**	**10,731**	**7,110**	**11,298**
以每间实际入住客房计算											
工资及相关开支	41	25	15	44	32	25	25	59	36	28	42
品牌系统市场推广费用	15	7	6	15	14	8	5	18	14	11	21
特许加盟费	16	7	14	16	18	8	4	17	14	3	32
其他开支	21	10	7	24	11	11	8	29	18	14	24
部门开支合计	**74**	**39**	**25**	**84**	**50**	**43**	**32**	**105**	**65**	**49**	**83**
以占总收入百分比计算											
工资及相关开支	3.3%	3.6%	3.3%	3.4%	3.1%	3.7%	3.4%	3.7%	3.2%	3.2%	2.8%
品牌系统市场推广费用	1.3%	1.0%	1.3%	1.2%	1.4%	1.2%	0.7%	1.2%	1.2%	1.3%	1.5%
特许加盟费	1.3%	1.0%	3.8%	1.2%	1.9%	1.2%	0.5%	1.1%	1.3%	0.3%	1.9%
其他开支	1.7%	1.4%	1.3%	1.8%	1.1%	1.6%	1.0%	1.8%	1.6%	1.6%	1.6%
部门开支合计	**6.0%**	**5.5%**	**5.4%**	**6.4%**	**4.9%**	**6.3%**	**4.5%**	**6.7%**	**5.8%**	**5.6%**	**5.6%**
物业营运及保养											
以每间可供出租客房计算	（元）	（元）	（元）	（元）	（元）	（元）	（元）	（元）	（元）	（元）	（元）
工资及相关开支	5,566	4,156	2,719	6,005	4,518	3,889	4,442	7,436	4,936	3,920	6,388
其他开支	5,856	3,804	1,792	6,406	4,476	3,536	3,935	8,523	4,701	3,770	7,665
部门开支合计	**11,410**	**7,722**	**4,129**	**12,453**	**8,896**	**7,386**	**7,912**	**16,046**	**9,624**	**7,615**	**13,951**
以每间实际入住客房计算											
工资及相关开支	36	26	16	38	31	24	28	50	30	27	47
其他开支	38	24	11	41	31	22	25	58	29	26	57
部门开支合计	**74**	**48**	**24**	**79**	**61**	**46**	**49**	**109**	**58**	**53**	**103**
以占总收入百分比计算											
工资及相关开支	2.9%	3.7%	3.6%	2.9%	3.0%	3.5%	3.9%	3.2%	2.7%	3.1%	3.1%
其他开支	3.1%	3.4%	2.3%	3.1%	3.0%	3.2%	3.4%	3.7%	2.6%	3.0%	3.8%
部门开支合计	**6.0%**	**6.8%**	**5.4%**	**6.0%**	**6.0%**	**6.7%**	**6.9%**	**7.0%**	**5.2%**	**6.0%**	**6.9%**

备注 Notes:

1. 纵向合计将不会完全符合，所有平均数据只平均为该行提供数据的酒店。
   Vertical totals will not always add up since averages were only based on hotels that contributed data to the specific line item.

	以平均房价分类 By Average Room Rate				以主要市场分类 By Key Market				
	¥ 1,000 以上 Above ¥ 1,000	¥ 701~1,000 Between ¥ 701-1,000	¥ 401~700 Between ¥ 401-700	¥ 400 及以下 Below ¥ 400	北京 Beijing 五星/5-Star	上海 Shanghai 五星/5-Star	广州 Guangzhou 五星/5-Star	深圳 Shenzhen 五星/5-Star	三亚 Sanya 五星/5-Star
Marketing									
Per Available Room	**RMB**	**RMB**	**RMB**	**RMB**	**RMB**	**RMB**	**RMB**	**RMB**	**RMB**
Payroll & Related Expenses	10,522	7,971	5,421	3,350	8,786	8,623	8,456	8,408	7,265
Centralized Chain Marketing	4,613	2,813	1,787	1,045	2,461	2,485	3,064	3,844	3,937
Franchise Fees	4,102	2,690	1,628	1,925	2,478	2,221	3,377	2,535	6,884
All Other Expenses	6,377	4,193	2,528	1,342	3,503	4,316	4,647	5,561	4,591
Total Departmental Expenses	**21,976**	**14,569**	**9,310**	**5,263**	**14,269**	**15,770**	**15,780**	**16,904**	**16,010**
Per Occupied Room									
Payroll & Related Expenses	74	53	34	21	74	57	47	53	43
Centralized Chain Marketing	32	18	11	6	20	16	16	24	23
Franchise Fees	29	17	10	11	21	15	17	18	37
All Other Expenses	45	28	16	9	30	28	26	35	27
Total Departmental Expenses	**154**	**96**	**59**	**33**	**121**	**104**	**88**	**107**	**95**
% of Total Revenue									
Payroll & Related Expenses	2.9%	3.5%	3.5%	3.4%	4.4%	4.0%	2.8%	3.2%	2.4%
Centralized Chain Marketing	1.3%	1.2%	1.2%	1.1%	1.2%	1.2%	1.0%	1.4%	1.3%
Franchise Fees	1.1%	1.2%	1.1%	2.0%	1.2%	1.0%	1.1%	1.0%	2.3%
All Other Expenses	1.7%	1.8%	1.6%	1.4%	1.7%	2.0%	1.5%	2.1%	1.5%
Total Departmental Expenses	**6.0%**	**6.3%**	**6.0%**	**5.4%**	**7.1%**	**7.3%**	**5.2%**	**6.4%**	**5.3%**
Property Operations & Maintenance									
Per Available Room	**RMB**	**RMB**	**RMB**	**RMB**	**RMB**	**RMB**	**RMB**	**RMB**	**RMB**
Payroll & Related Expenses	9,450	6,695	4,952	3,369	8,216	6,992	7,677	7,025	8,524
All Other Expenses	11,300	7,407	4,798	3,000	10,848	7,539	9,107	6,878	11,235
Total Departmental Expenses	**20,961**	**14,081**	**9,680**	**6,152**	**18,939**	**14,851**	**16,784**	**13,894**	**19,759**
Per Occupied Room									
Payroll & Related Expenses	66	44	31	21	69	46	42	44	51
All Other Expenses	79	49	30	19	92	50	50	44	67
Total Departmental Expenses	**147**	**93**	**61**	**38**	**160**	**98**	**93**	**88**	**118**
% of Total Revenue									
Payroll & Related Expenses	2.6%	2.9%	3.2%	3.4%	4.1%	3.2%	2.5%	2.6%	2.8%
All Other Expenses	3.1%	3.2%	3.1%	3.1%	5.4%	3.5%	3.0%	2.6%	3.7%
Total Departmental Expenses	**5.7%**	**6.1%**	**6.3%**	**6.3%**	**9.4%**	**6.9%**	**5.5%**	**5.2%**	**6.5%**

表 7 客源构成

	以星级分类 By Star Rating			以管理模式分类 By Management Model				以城市等级分类 By City Category			
	五星 5-Star	四星 4-Star	三星+有限服务 3-Star + Limited Service	国际管理 International 五星/5-Star	国内管理 Domestic 五星/5-Star	国际管理 International 四星/4-Star	国内管理 Domestic 四星/4-Star	一线城市 Tier 1 cities 五星/5-Star	二线城市 Tier 2 cities 五星/5-Star	三线城市 Tier 3 cities 五星/5-Star	目的地度假村 Destination Resort 五星/5-Star
客源构成											
市场分布											
散客 - 商务散客	29.1%	27.1%	29.7%	31.2%	24.0%	31.3%	22.0%	30.8%	32.6%	30.7%	9.1%
散客 - 直接散客	26.9%	17.8%	17.5%	29.9%	19.6%	18.9%	16.5%	33.3%	25.4%	19.8%	29.1%
散客 - 批发/包价散客	8.6%	6.1%	5.8%	8.4%	8.9%	5.2%	7.5%	8.1%	6.5%	5.8%	21.6%
团队 - 酒店店内会议	14.5%	17.6%	13.2%	12.8%	19.0%	14.0%	22.5%	12.5%	15.3%	16.1%	13.1%
团队 - 会议/会展/会奖旅游	4.2%	4.9%	2.7%	3.9%	4.8%	5.4%	4.3%	2.7%	4.2%	4.3%	6.2%
团队 - 旅游团队	2.3%	2.8%	3.7%	2.0%	2.8%	2.9%	2.7%	1.3%	1.8%	2.1%	6.4%
无预订散客	3.1%	3.0%	5.4%	3.3%	2.6%	3.4%	2.5%	2.4%	3.2%	4.1%	2.7%
政府散客	7.3%	13.0%	14.5%	4.5%	14.1%	11.0%	14.3%	4.0%	7.0%	13.6%	7.6%
航空机组人员	0.6%	1.9%	0.5%	0.6%	0.3%	1.7%	2.2%	0.9%	0.6%	0.3%	0.2%
其他	3.5%	5.9%	6.9%	3.5%	3.8%	6.3%	5.3%	4.0%	3.3%	3.2%	4.0%
合计	**100.0%**	**100.0%**	**100.0%**	**100.0%**	**100.0%**	**100.0%**	**100.0%**	**100.0%**	**100.0%**	**100.0%**	**100.0%**
订房渠道											
酒店协议客户	42.2%	50.7%	45.6%	38.1%	52.2%	47.7%	54.6%	35.2%	45.6%	55.9%	25.6%
电话/邮件/上门散客	11.5%	10.5%	9.8%	11.1%	12.3%	10.7%	10.2%	12.4%	11.2%	11.8%	10.5%
酒店社交媒体	2.3%	1.8%	1.8%	2.3%	2.1%	1.7%	1.7%	1.9%	2.0%	1.7%	4.8%
酒店管理集团线上渠道	10.2%	9.3%	16.7%	11.9%	6.4%	11.3%	6.8%	11.8%	10.3%	7.4%	10.0%
酒店管理集团线下渠道	5.3%	5.3%	4.2%	6.5%	2.5%	4.9%	5.4%	7.0%	5.3%	2.9%	4.8%
OTA直连	21.3%	16.6%	16.1%	22.1%	19.2%	16.2%	17.2%	24.2%	20.1%	16.6%	26.3%
非直连分销商（旅行社／旅游运营商）	4.8%	4.8%	5.1%	4.6%	5.0%	5.3%	4.0%	3.6%	2.9%	2.9%	17.1%
国际订房系统	2.5%	1.2%	0.8%	3.4%	0.3%	2.1%	0.1%	3.9%	2.7%	0.9%	1.0%
合计	**100.0%**	**100.0%**	**100.0%**	**100.0%**	**100.0%**	**100.0%**	**100.0%**	**100.0%**	**100.0%**	**100.0%**	**100.0%**
以客源国 / 地区计算											
亚洲	**97.6%**	**98.3%**	**98.9%**	**96.8%**	**99.3%**	**97.8%**	**99.1%**	**94.8%**	**98.1%**	**99.1%**	**98.6%**
中国大陆	94.9%	95.2%	96.1%	93.6%	97.8%	94.1%	96.7%	91.2%	95.4%	97.1%	96.6%
中国香港	0.8%	0.7%	0.8%	0.9%	0.4%	0.7%	0.8%	1.3%	0.6%	0.7%	0.6%
印度	0.0%	0.0%	0.0%	0.0%	0.0%	0.1%	0.0%	0.0%	0.0%	0.0%	0.0%
日本	0.5%	0.8%	0.7%	0.6%	0.2%	1.2%	0.5%	0.6%	0.6%	0.2%	0.1%
韩国	0.5%	0.4%	0.2%	0.6%	0.2%	0.6%	0.1%	0.4%	0.6%	0.4%	0.2%
中国台湾	0.4%	0.5%	0.5%	0.4%	0.4%	0.4%	0.6%	0.4%	0.5%	0.4%	0.2%
东南亚	0.2%	0.2%	0.2%	0.2%	0.1%	0.2%	0.1%	0.3%	0.2%	0.1%	0.1%
亚洲其他地区	0.4%	0.4%	0.4%	0.4%	0.3%	0.4%	0.4%	0.5%	0.2%	0.2%	0.8%
北美洲	**0.8%**	**0.5%**	**0.3%**	**1.1%**	**0.2%**	**0.8%**	**0.3%**	**1.7%**	**0.7%**	**0.5%**	**0.4%**
加拿大	0.1%	0.1%	0.1%	0.1%	0.1%	0.1%	0.1%	0.2%	0.1%	0.0%	0.1%
墨西哥	0.0%	0.0%	0.0%	0.0%	0.0%	0.0%	0.0%	0.0%	0.0%	0.0%	0.0%
美国	0.7%	0.4%	0.3%	1.0%	0.1%	0.6%	0.2%	1.5%	0.5%	0.4%	0.3%
中南美洲	**0.1%**	**0.1%**	**0.1%**	**0.1%**	**0.0%**	**0.1%**	**0.1%**	**0.1%**	**0.1%**	**0.0%**	**0.1%**
欧洲	**0.6%**	**0.5%**	**0.4%**	**0.8%**	**0.2%**	**0.7%**	**0.2%**	**1.1%**	**0.6%**	**0.2%**	**0.4%**
中/东欧	0.0%	0.1%	0.0%	0.0%	0.0%	0.1%	0.0%	0.1%	0.0%	0.0%	0.0%
法国	0.1%	0.1%	0.1%	0.1%	0.0%	0.1%	0.0%	0.1%	0.1%	0.0%	0.0%
德国	0.2%	0.1%	0.1%	0.3%	0.1%	0.2%	0.0%	0.3%	0.2%	0.1%	0.2%
意大利	0.1%	0.0%	0.0%	0.1%	0.0%	0.1%	0.0%	0.1%	0.1%	0.0%	0.0%
斯堪的纳维亚	0.0%	0.0%	0.0%	0.0%	0.0%	0.0%	0.0%	0.0%	0.0%	0.0%	0.0%
西班牙	0.0%	0.0%	0.0%	0.0%	0.0%	0.0%	0.0%	0.1%	0.0%	0.0%	0.0%
英国	0.1%	0.1%	0.1%	0.1%	0.0%	0.1%	0.1%	0.2%	0.1%	0.0%	0.1%
欧洲其他地区（含俄罗斯）	0.1%	0.1%	0.1%	0.1%	0.0%	0.1%	0.0%	0.2%	0.1%	0.1%	0.1%
中东	**0.0%**	**0.0%**	**0.0%**	**0.0%**	**0.0%**	**0.0%**	**0.0%**	**0.1%**	**0.0%**	**0.0%**	**0.0%**
非洲	**0.0%**	**0.0%**	**0.1%**	**0.0%**	**0.0%**	**0.0%**	**0.0%**	**0.1%**	**0.0%**	**0.0%**	**0.0%**
澳大利亚	**0.1%**	**0.1%**	**0.0%**	**0.1%**	**0.1%**	**0.1%**	**0.0%**	**0.1%**	**0.1%**	**0.0%**	**0.0%**
新西兰	**0.0%**	**0.0%**	**0.1%**	**0.0%**	**0.0%**	**0.0%**	**0.0%**	**0.1%**	**0.0%**	**0.0%**	**0.0%**
其他	**0.7%**	**0.4%**	**0.1%**	**1.0%**	**0.1%**	**0.5%**	**0.2%**	**1.9%**	**0.5%**	**0.1%**	**0.4%**
总合计	**100.0%**	**100.0%**	**100.0%**	**100.0%**	**100.0%**	**100.0%**	**100.0%**	**100.0%**	**100.0%**	**100.0%**	**100.0%**

TABLE 7 GUEST PROFILE

	以平均房价分类 By Average Room Rate				以主要市场分类 By Key Market				
	¥ 1,000 以上 Above ¥ 1,000	¥ 701~1,000 Between ¥ 701-1,000	¥ 401~700 Between ¥ 401-700	¥ 400 及以下 Below ¥ 400	北京 Beijing 五星/5-Star	上海 Shanghai 五星/5-Star	广州 Guangzhou 五星/5-Star	深圳 Shenzhen 五星/5-Star	三亚 Sanya 五星/5-Star
Guest Profile									
By Market Segmentation									
Transient - Corporate/Business FIT	20.0%	29.7%	33.1%	24.8%	32.5%	26.9%	30.5%	32.7%	5.5%
Transient - Direct FIT	40.9%	34.5%	24.4%	15.9%	32.9%	29.3%	39.9%	34.2%	35.2%
Transient - Wholesale/Package FIT	16.2%	10.2%	7.2%	5.8%	7.0%	10.6%	6.7%	8.8%	29.8%
Group - In-house Meeting	9.5%	9.0%	14.0%	20.1%	12.6%	14.4%	11.2%	11.2%	7.2%
Group - Other MICE	3.7%	3.5%	3.9%	5.0%	3.3%	3.2%	2.2%	1.6%	6.9%
Group - Leisure Group	2.0%	2.1%	2.3%	3.0%	0.7%	2.3%	0.7%	1.1%	2.7%
Other - Walk-in	2.8%	2.8%	3.1%	3.7%	1.7%	2.5%	1.9%	4.4%	2.8%
Other - Government	1.3%	3.0%	6.9%	16.1%	3.5%	5.3%	3.3%	2.9%	7.0%
Other - Airline	0.1%	0.4%	0.9%	1.0%	0.4%	0.9%	1.6%	0.7%	0.0%
Other, Specify	3.5%	4.6%	4.2%	4.7%	5.3%	4.6%	2.0%	2.2%	2.8%
Total	**100.0%**	**100.0%**	**100.0%**	**100.0%**	**100.0%**	**100.0%**	**100.0%**	**100.0%**	**100.0%**
By Source of Advanced Reservation									
Corporate Account	20.0%	29.7%	45.3%	54.2%	38.4%	34.9%	33.0%	28.0%	18.0%
FIT Telephone/Email Booking/Walk-in	13.5%	11.5%	10.5%	11.2%	12.4%	11.7%	13.9%	11.6%	10.7%
Property's Social Media Platform	2.6%	2.7%	2.1%	1.7%	2.6%	2.2%	1.2%	2.1%	4.1%
Hotel Management Group Online Channel	13.3%	13.6%	10.6%	8.7%	11.2%	11.0%	11.3%	15.2%	10.5%
Hotel Management Group Offline Channel	7.1%	7.9%	5.5%	3.4%	6.9%	7.3%	5.7%	9.4%	3.4%
OTA	29.8%	25.2%	19.6%	15.8%	21.3%	24.4%	27.3%	25.3%	32.7%
Wholesaler (Travel Agent / Tour Operator)	8.8%	6.2%	4.0%	4.4%	4.2%	3.8%	5.2%	4.0%	19.5%
Global Distribution System (GDS)	5.1%	3.3%	2.3%	0.6%	3.0%	4.9%	2.5%	4.4%	1.2%
Total	**100.0%**	**100.0%**	**100.0%**	**100.0%**	**100.0%**	**100.0%**	**100.0%**	**100.0%**	**100.0%**
By Country of Origin									
ASIA	**96.5%**	**95.9%**	**97.7%**	**99.0%**	**96.1%**	**94.3%**	**96.3%**	**92.2%**	**97.4%**
China Mainland	93.2%	93.2%	94.5%	96.9%	93.5%	91.5%	90.9%	87.1%	95.1%
Hong Kong SAR, China	1.4%	1.0%	0.7%	0.6%	0.9%	1.0%	1.3%	2.6%	0.3%
India	0.0%	0.0%	0.0%	0.0%	0.0%	0.0%	0.1%	0.1%	0.0%
Japan	0.3%	0.2%	0.8%	0.5%	0.3%	0.5%	1.2%	0.3%	0.1%
Korea	0.3%	0.4%	0.5%	0.3%	0.4%	0.3%	0.7%	0.5%	0.1%
Taiwan Prov., China	0.4%	0.4%	0.5%	0.4%	0.3%	0.4%	0.3%	0.7%	0.1%
South East Asia	0.3%	0.3%	0.2%	0.1%	0.3%	0.3%	0.2%	0.4%	0.1%
Other Asian	0.8%	0.4%	0.4%	0.2%	0.3%	0.2%	1.6%	0.5%	1.5%
NORTH AMERICA	**1.5%**	**1.5%**	**0.7%**	**0.3%**	**1.6%**	**2.0%**	**1.3%**	**1.5%**	**0.5%**
Canada	0.2%	0.1%	0.1%	0.1%	0.2%	0.2%	0.1%	0.2%	0.1%
Mexico	0.0%	0.0%	0.0%	0.0%	0.0%	0.0%	0.0%	0.0%	0.0%
USA	1.3%	1.3%	0.6%	0.2%	1.4%	1.8%	1.2%	1.3%	0.4%
SOUTH & CENTRAL AMERICA	**0.1%**	**0.1%**	**0.1%**	**0.1%**	**0.1%**	**0.1%**	**0.1%**	**0.1%**	**0.2%**
EUROPE	**1.0%**	**0.9%**	**0.6%**	**0.3%**	**1.6%**	**1.2%**	**0.8%**	**0.6%**	**0.7%**
Central/Eastern Europe	0.1%	0.1%	0.0%	0.0%	0.1%	0.1%	0.1%	0.0%	0.0%
France	0.1%	0.1%	0.1%	0.0%	0.1%	0.1%	0.1%	0.1%	0.1%
Germany	0.2%	0.3%	0.2%	0.1%	0.5%	0.3%	0.2%	0.1%	0.2%
Italy	0.1%	0.1%	0.1%	0.0%	0.2%	0.1%	0.1%	0.1%	0.0%
Scandinavia	0.0%	0.0%	0.0%	0.0%	0.0%	0.1%	0.0%	0.0%	0.0%
Spain	0.1%	0.0%	0.0%	0.0%	0.2%	0.1%	0.0%	0.0%	0.0%
United Kingdom	0.2%	0.2%	0.1%	0.1%	0.3%	0.2%	0.2%	0.2%	0.1%
Other Europe (Inc. Russia)	0.2%	0.2%	0.1%	0.1%	0.2%	0.3%	0.1%	0.0%	0.2%
MIDDLE EAST	**0.0%**	**0.0%**	**0.0%**	**0.0%**	**0.1%**	**0.1%**	**0.1%**	**0.1%**	**0.0%**
AFRICA	**0.1%**	**0.0%**	**0.0%**	**0.0%**	**0.1%**	**0.0%**	**0.1%**	**0.0%**	**0.1%**
AUSTRALIA	**0.1%**	**0.1%**	**0.1%**	**0.0%**	**0.2%**	**0.1%**	**0.1%**	**0.1%**	**0.1%**
NEW ZEALAND	**0.0%**	**0.0%**	**0.0%**	**0.0%**	**0.0%**	**0.1%**	**0.0%**	**0.0%**	**0.0%**
OTHERS	**0.6%**	**1.5%**	**0.7%**	**0.2%**	**0.2%**	**2.2%**	**1.1%**	**5.3%**	**1.0%**
GRAND TOTAL	**100.0%**	**100.0%**	**100.0%**	**100.0%**	**100.0%**	**100.0%**	**100.0%**	**100.0%**	**100.0%**

表 8　餐饮统计

	以星级分类 By Star Rating			以管理模式分类 By Management Model				以城市等级分类 By City Category			
	五星 5-Star	四星 4-Star	三星+有限服务 3-Star + Limited Service	国际管理 International 五星/5-Star	国内管理 Domestic 五星/5-Star	国际管理 International 四星/4-Star	国内管理 Domestic 四星/4-Star	一线城市 Tier 1 cities 五星/5-Star	二线城市 Tier 2 cities 五星/5-Star	三线城市 Tier 3 cities 五星/5-Star	目的地度假村 Destination Resort 五星/5-Star
餐饮设施及营运指标											
每间可供出租客房均摊餐位数											
全日咖啡厅	0.54	0.55	0.54	0.54	0.54	0.52	0.57	0.48	0.52	0.55	0.70
中餐厅	0.60	0.64	0.54	0.53	0.73	0.52	0.78	0.51	0.58	0.80	0.61
西餐/特色餐厅	0.29	0.30	N/A	0.29	0.28	0.24	0.32	0.28	0.28	0.27	0.36
大堂吧/酒吧	0.25	0.19	0.19	0.27	0.20	0.19	0.17	0.29	0.25	0.18	0.28
合计	**1.68**	**1.69**	**1.26**	**1.64**	**1.75**	**1.47**	**1.84**	**1.56**	**1.63**	**1.80**	**1.95**
每间可供出租客房均摊宴会/会议设施面积 (平方米)	**6.00**	**4.62**	**2.23**	**5.58**	**6.91**	**4.10**	**5.26**	**5.45**	**6.16**	**7.29**	**5.08**
每间实际入住客房均摊餐位上座数											
全日咖啡厅	1.30	1.19	1.21	1.35	1.18	1.21	1.12	1.11	1.29	1.26	1.73
中餐厅	0.57	0.66	0.72	0.46	0.79	0.54	0.80	0.57	0.51	0.82	0.53
西餐/特色餐厅	0.23	0.41	N/A	0.21	0.28	0.21	0.53	0.27	0.19	0.18	0.37
大堂吧/酒吧	0.17	0.08	0.10	0.19	0.13	0.07	0.10	0.24	0.15	0.07	0.25
客房送餐服务	0.07	0.06	0.16	0.07	0.08	0.06	0.09	0.09	0.06	0.07	0.09
宴会/会议	0.48	0.36	0.45	0.41	0.67	0.29	0.48	0.34	0.51	0.81	0.30
每日每餐位平均上座数											
全日咖啡厅	1.03	0.96	1.08	1.10	0.88	1.04	0.86	0.95	1.13	0.93	0.94
中餐厅	0.41	0.45	0.54	0.38	0.45	0.46	0.45	0.46	0.41	0.41	0.33
西餐/特色餐厅	0.35	0.59	N/A	0.32	0.41	0.42	0.70	0.40	0.31	0.27	0.41
大堂吧/酒吧	0.29	0.18	0.19	0.30	0.27	0.16	0.22	0.34	0.27	0.16	0.34
人均餐饮消费	（元）	（元）	（元）	（元）	（元）	（元）	（元）	（元）	（元）	（元）	（元）
全日咖啡厅	96	63	51	99	85	60	67	122	92	73	94
中餐厅	215	148	109	256	162	149	147	271	225	147	189
西餐/特色餐厅	216	92	N/A	237	145	139	82	259	210	128	187
大堂吧/酒吧	129	74	47	138	91	72	80	163	124	78	99
客房送餐服务	102	61	56	117	57	59	65	131	89	68	121
宴会/会议	344	233	181	416	232	262	204	548	340	218	332
合计 (平均)	**171**	**106**	**62**	**184**	**142**	**102**	**111**	**225**	**171**	**133**	**138**

备注 Notes:

1. 纵向合计将不会完全符合，所有平均数据只平均为该行提供数据的酒店。
   Vertical totals will not always add up since averages were only based on hotels that contributed data to the specific line item.

TABLE 8 FOOD & BEVERAGE STATISTICS

	以平均房价分类 By Average Room Rate				以主要市场分类 By Key Market				
	¥ 1,000 以上 Above ¥ 1,000	¥ 701~1,000 Between ¥ 701-1,000	¥ 401~700 Between ¥ 401-700	¥ 400 及以下 Below ¥ 400	北京 Beijing 五星/5-Star	上海 Shanghai 五星/5-Star	广州 Guangzhou 五星/5-Star	深圳 Shenzhen 五星/5-Star	三亚 Sanya 五星/5-Star
Food & Beverage Operation									
Seat Per Available Room									
Coffee Shop	0.61	0.55	0.52	0.54	0.46	0.48	0.48	0.54	0.69
Chinese	0.55	0.52	0.59	0.71	0.42	0.47	0.65	0.65	0.43
Western/Specialty	0.37	0.32	0.24	0.29	0.29	0.25	0.26	0.36	0.38
Lounge/Bar	0.44	0.30	0.20	0.19	0.26	0.28	0.30	0.35	0.27
Total	**1.96**	**1.69**	**1.56**	**1.72**	**1.44**	**1.47**	**1.70**	**1.90**	**1.76**
Function Space Per Available Room (SQM)	**5.61**	**5.60**	**5.55**	**5.26**	**5.09**	**4.73**	**7.80**	**5.70**	**4.55**
Covers Per Occupied Room									
Coffee Shop	1.65	1.41	1.24	1.16	1.12	1.07	1.19	1.34	1.50
Chinese	0.57	0.49	0.55	0.70	0.49	0.39	0.90	0.65	0.33
Western/Specialty	0.38	0.25	0.19	0.24	0.32	0.24	0.17	0.49	0.40
Lounge/Bar	0.43	0.24	0.11	0.07	0.32	0.17	0.30	0.28	0.26
Room Service	0.14	0.07	0.07	0.06	0.10	0.07	0.11	0.07	0.13
Banquet & Function	0.37	0.40	0.45	0.51	0.21	0.35	0.41	0.43	0.07
Seating Turnover Per Day									
Coffee Shop	1.06	1.08	1.05	0.94	0.80	0.93	1.22	1.08	1.01
Chinese	0.42	0.41	0.41	0.43	0.38	0.37	0.68	0.43	0.36
Western/Specialty	0.42	0.33	0.35	0.37	0.34	0.37	0.35	0.61	0.47
Lounge/Bar	0.39	0.34	0.23	0.18	0.39	0.26	0.48	0.35	0.43
Average F&B Check Per Cover	**RMB**	**RMB**	**RMB**	**RMB**	**RMB**	**RMB**	**RMB**	**RMB**	**RMB**
Coffee Shop	148	110	81	61	112	105	145	140	103
Chinese	407	283	190	130	265	288	246	306	231
Western/Specialty	287	217	174	115	282	247	357	181	212
Lounge/Bar	191	116	88	74	135	160	203	127	114
Room Service	171	113	72	53	145	135	108	137	132
Banquet & Function	634	472	319	207	517	596	471	567	732
Total (Average)	**258**	**197**	**148**	**106**	**186**	**230**	**231**	**240**	**150**

表 9　人事统计

	以星级分类 By Star Rating			以管理模式分类 By Management Model				以城市等级分类 By City Category			
	五星 5-Star	四星 4-Star	三星+有限服务 3-Star + Limited Service	国际管理 International 五星/5-Star	国内管理 Domestic 五星/5-Star	国际管理 International 四星/4-Star	国内管理 Domestic 四星/4-Star	一线城市 Tier 1 cities 五星/5-Star	二线城市 Tier 2 cities 五星/5-Star	三线城市 Tier 3 cities 五星/5-Star	目的地度假村 Destination Resort 五星/5-Star
工资及相关开支											
以每间可供出租客房计算	（元）	（元）	（元）	（元）	（元）	（元）	（元）	（元）	（元）	（元）	（元）
客房	15,183	11,160	9,458	16,485	12,047	10,980	11,255	19,563	14,196	10,613	15,964
餐饮	29,186	16,070	6,452	31,871	22,879	15,354	17,127	40,231	27,564	20,607	25,137
水疗及健身	2,484	1,451	1,396	2,586	2,156	1,218	2,078	2,978	1,828	1,355	4,428
其他营运部门	2,509	3,285	3,424	1,851	3,724	1,418	5,664	3,228	2,150	2,409	2,727
行政	17,638	12,675	7,616	18,134	16,176	11,545	13,922	24,071	16,023	13,424	17,101
信息及通信系统	1,275	887	526	1,319	764	823	689	1,545	1,251	787	1,166
市场推广	6,245	4,045	2,510	6,948	4,666	4,070	3,941	8,626	5,877	4,084	5,699
物业营运及保养	5,566	4,156	2,719	6,005	4,518	3,889	4,442	7,436	4,936	3,920	6,388
工资及相关开支合计	**80,086**	**53,728**	**34,099**	**85,200**	**66,930**	**49,298**	**59,117**	**107,678**	**73,826**	**57,200**	**78,611**
以每间实际入住客房计算	（元）	（元）	（元）	（元）	（元）	（元）	（元）	（元）	（元）	（元）	（元）
客房	99	69	57	104	82	68	70	133	86	73	117
餐饮	189	99	38	202	156	95	107	274	167	143	185
水疗及健身	16	9	9	16	15	8	16	19	11	10	32
其他营运部门	16	20	20	12	26	9	36	22	13	16	20
行政	114	78	46	115	111	71	88	164	97	93	126
信息及通信系统	8	5	3	8	5	5	4	10	8	5	9
市场推广	41	25	15	44	32	25	25	59	36	28	42
物业营运及保养	36	26	16	38	31	24	28	50	30	27	47
以占收入百分比计算											
客房	15.1%	17.2%	16.5%	14.3%	17.6%	15.6%	19.6%	16.6%	15.0%	17.9%	11.8%
餐饮	38.8%	43.1%	42.1%	39.9%	35.3%	44.6%	42.4%	46.3%	34.9%	33.9%	44.0%
水疗及健身	60.1%	55.4%	78.6%	64.1%	48.7%	64.6%	42.8%	53.3%	54.1%	49.9%	85.2%
其他营运部门	57.2%	41.1%	57.6%	68.3%	47.1%	70.4%	37.2%	45.0%	58.9%	65.5%	81.3%
行政	9.3%	11.2%	10.0%	8.8%	10.8%	10.5%	12.1%	10.4%	8.7%	10.6%	8.4%
信息及通信系统	0.7%	0.8%	0.7%	0.6%	0.5%	0.8%	0.6%	0.7%	0.7%	0.6%	0.6%
市场推广	3.3%	3.6%	3.3%	3.4%	3.1%	3.7%	3.4%	3.7%	3.2%	3.2%	2.8%
物业营运及保养	2.9%	3.7%	3.6%	2.9%	3.0%	3.5%	3.9%	3.2%	2.7%	3.1%	3.1%
占总收入百分比	**42.3%**	**47.5%**	**44.6%**	**41.1%**	**44.8%**	**45.0%**	**51.3%**	**46.7%**	**40.1%**	**45.1%**	**38.7%**

平均工资水平 – 前线员工（按星级分类）
Average Salary Scale - Rank & File Positions (By Star Rating)

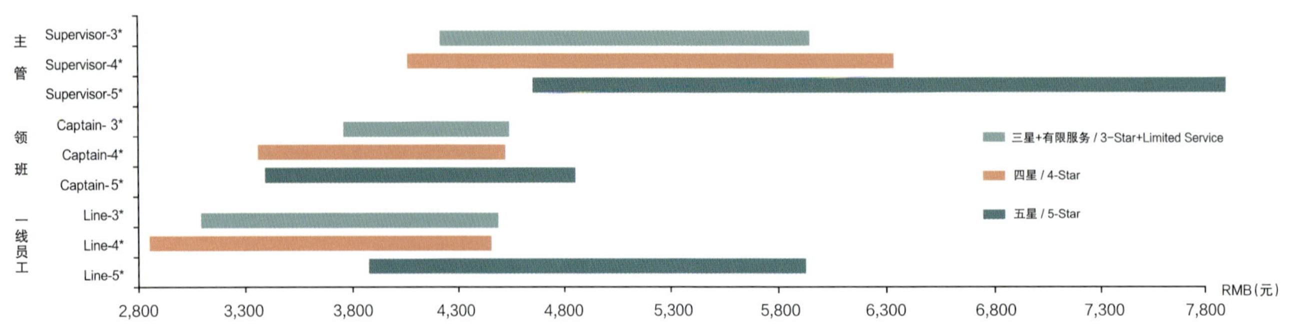

备注 Notes:

1. 纵向合计将不会完全符合，所有平均数据只平均为该行提供数据的酒店。
   Vertical totals will not always add up since averages were only applied to hotels that contributed data to the specific line item.
2. 各部门支出百分比以其部门收入为基础，其他未分配部门以总收入为基础。
   Expense ratios for departmental expenses are based on their respective departmental revenues, all other expenses are based on total revenue.

	以平均房价分类 By Average Room Rate				以主要市场分类 By Key Market				
	¥ 1,000 以上 Above ¥ 1,000	¥ 701~1,000 Between ¥ 701-1,000	¥ 401~700 Between ¥ 401-700	¥ 400 及以下 Below ¥ 400	北京 Beijing 五星/5-Star	上海 Shanghai 五星/5-Star	广州 Guangzhou 五星/5-Star	深圳 Shenzhen 五星/5-Star	三亚 Sanya 五星/5-Star
Payroll & Related Expenses									
Per Available Room	**RMB**	**RMB**	**RMB**	**RMB**	**RMB**	**RMB**	**RMB**	**RMB**	**RMB**
Rooms	25,787	18,616	13,424	9,472	20,060	19,229	19,811	20,249	20,307
Food & Beverage	52,924	36,264	23,621	14,486	38,073	38,722	44,596	44,713	32,089
Spa & Fitness Center	5,621	2,685	1,641	1,243	3,378	2,804	2,940	3,214	6,927
Other Operated Depts.	3,119	2,892	2,594	2,573	4,281	2,556	3,099	3,771	3,227
Administrative & General	28,539	21,543	15,502	10,761	28,793	21,666	22,874	20,734	20,543
Information & Telecommunications	2,107	1,472	1,034	762	1,594	1,388	1,728	1,640	1,300
Marketing	10,522	7,971	5,421	3,350	8,786	8,623	8,456	8,408	7,265
Property Operations & Maintenance	9,450	6,695	4,952	3,369	8,216	6,992	7,677	7,025	8,524
Total Payroll and Related Exp.	**138,069**	**98,139**	**68,189**	**46,015**	**113,181**	**101,980**	**111,181**	**109,755**	**100,184**
Per Occupied Room	**RMB**	**RMB**	**RMB**	**RMB**	**RMB**	**RMB**	**RMB**	**RMB**	**RMB**
Rooms	181	123	84	59	170	126	111	128	121
Food & Beverage	372	239	149	90	324	255	249	283	191
Spa & Fitness Center	39	18	10	8	28	18	15	20	42
Other Operated Depts.	22	19	17	16	41	17	18	23	20
Administrative & General	200	142	98	68	245	142	128	131	123
Information & Telecommunications	15	9	6	5	13	9	9	10	8
Marketing	74	53	34	21	74	57	47	53	43
Property Operations & Maintenance	66	44	31	21	69	46	42	44	51
% of Revenue									
Rooms	12.3%	15.0%	16.1%	18.1%	18.4%	16.2%	14.8%	14.6%	9.0%
Food & Beverage	40.5%	41.2%	39.1%	37.3%	67.4%	49.0%	32.1%	38.8%	49.0%
Spa & Fitness Center	65.5%	58.6%	55.2%	53.8%	42.3%	68.9%	50.8%	67.1%	175.9%
Other Operated Depts.	56.3%	66.5%	51.0%	46.1%	43.2%	67.4%	27.3%	113.8%	149.2%
Administrative & General	7.8%	9.3%	10.0%	11.0%	14.3%	10.1%	7.5%	7.8%	6.8%
Information & Telecommunications	0.6%	0.6%	0.7%	0.8%	0.8%	0.6%	0.6%	0.6%	0.4%
Marketing	2.9%	3.5%	3.5%	3.4%	4.4%	4.0%	2.8%	3.2%	2.4%
Property Operations & Maintenance	2.6%	2.9%	3.2%	3.4%	4.1%	3.2%	2.5%	2.6%	2.8%
As % of Total Revenue	**37.9%**	**42.5%**	**44.0%**	**46.9%**	**56.2%**	**47.3%**	**36.5%**	**41.2%**	**33.1%**

平均工资水平 – 管理阶层（按星级分类）
Average Salary Scale - Supervisory Positions (By Star Rating)

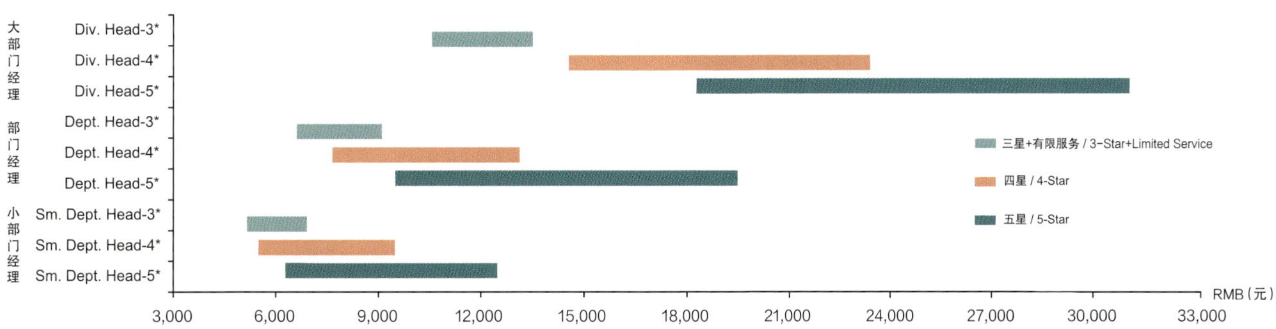

表 9　人事统计（续）

	以星级分类 By Star Rating			以管理模式分类 By Management Model				以城市等级分类 By City Category			
	五星 5-Star	四星 4-Star	三星+有限服务 3-Star + Limited Service	国际管理 International 五星/5-Star	国内管理 Domestic 五星/5-Star	国际管理 International 四星/4-Star	国内管理 Domestic 四星/4-Star	一线城市 Tier 1 cities 五星/5-Star	二线城市 Tier 2 cities 五星/5-Star	三线城市 Tier 3 cities 五星/5-Star	目的地度假村 Destination Resort 五星/5-Star
员工效率											
全酒店-按每间可供出租房分摊员工数	**0.88**	**0.59**	**0.38**	**0.90**	**0.83**	**0.56**	**0.60**	**0.92**	**0.85**	**0.82**	**0.96**
全职员工	0.66	0.46	0.27	0.67	0.63	0.43	0.48	0.70	0.65	0.63	0.68
临时/兼职员工	0.12	0.07	0.08	0.12	0.13	0.07	0.08	0.13	0.10	0.12	0.15
实习生	0.10	0.05	0.03	0.10	0.08	0.05	0.04	0.09	0.10	0.06	0.12
全酒店-按每间实际入住房分摊员工数	**2.08**	**1.32**	**0.81**	**2.07**	**2.08**	**1.25**	**1.37**	**2.29**	**1.89**	**2.05**	**2.56**
全职员工	1.57	1.03	0.57	1.56	1.56	0.97	1.09	1.74	1.44	1.60	1.83
临时/兼职员工	0.28	0.17	0.18	0.27	0.32	0.16	0.17	0.33	0.22	0.30	0.41
实习生	0.23	0.11	0.07	0.24	0.20	0.12	0.10	0.22	0.22	0.16	0.33
客房部-按每间实际入住房分摊工时	**3.26**	**2.26**	**2.11**	**3.25**	**3.24**	**2.18**	**2.31**	**3.42**	**2.95**	**3.20**	**4.36**
全职员工	2.25	1.63	1.30	2.22	2.27	1.54	1.71	2.35	2.07	2.39	2.75
临时/兼职员工	0.66	0.42	0.61	0.67	0.64	0.43	0.41	0.70	0.55	0.58	1.07
实习生	0.35	0.20	0.19	0.36	0.33	0.21	0.18	0.36	0.33	0.22	0.54
全酒店-按每间实际入住房分摊工时	**11.40**	**7.22**	**4.45**	**11.33**	**11.38**	**6.87**	**7.50**	**12.57**	**10.34**	**11.26**	**14.05**
全职员工	8.62	5.67	3.10	8.55	8.55	5.33	5.99	9.56	7.88	8.76	10.02
临时/兼职员工	1.53	0.92	0.98	1.47	1.74	0.89	0.96	1.80	1.23	1.63	2.24
实习生	1.25	0.63	0.36	1.31	1.09	0.66	0.56	1.22	1.22	0.87	1.80
餐饮部-每餐位分摊员工数	**0.18**	**0.14**	**0.12**	**0.19**	**0.15**	**0.14**	**0.14**	**0.20**	**0.18**	**0.15**	**0.16**
全职员工	0.13	0.11	0.10	0.14	0.11	0.11	0.11	0.15	0.13	0.11	0.11
临时/兼职员工	0.01	0.01	0.01	0.01	0.01	0.01	0.01	0.02	0.01	0.01	0.01
实习生	0.03	0.02	0.01	0.04	0.02	0.02	0.01	0.03	0.04	0.02	0.03
餐饮部-每用餐人次分摊工时	**1.63**	**0.97**	**0.47**	**1.70**	**1.49**	**1.02**	**0.95**	**2.01**	**1.58**	**1.45**	**1.51**
全职员工	1.09	0.67	0.28	1.15	0.97	0.69	0.66	1.39	1.05	0.98	0.96
临时/兼职员工	0.26	0.16	0.12	0.25	0.29	0.16	0.16	0.33	0.23	0.28	0.23
实习生	0.28	0.15	0.08	0.30	0.23	0.17	0.13	0.29	0.29	0.19	0.31
宴会部-每用餐人次分摊工时	**1.85**	**1.90**	**1.73**	**2.08**	**1.51**	**1.98**	**1.74**	**2.81**	**1.71**	**1.34**	**2.25**
全职员工	0.89	0.99	0.77	0.98	0.75	1.04	0.90	1.48	0.78	0.71	1.05
临时/兼职员工	0.73	0.59	0.79	0.86	0.54	0.57	0.59	1.01	0.72	0.46	0.89
实习生	0.23	0.31	0.17	0.23	0.23	0.36	0.25	0.33	0.21	0.17	0.32

平均工资水平 – 前线员工（按管理模式分类 – 五星级酒店）
Average Salary Scale - Rank & File Positions (By Management Model - 5-Star)

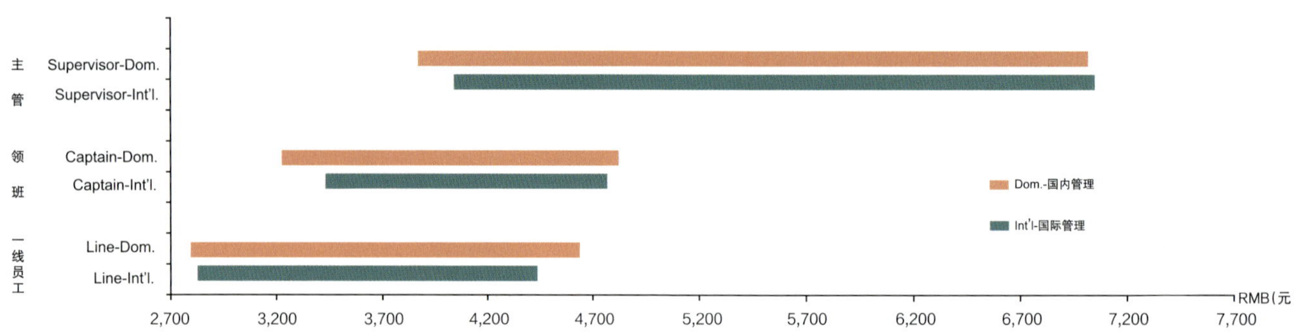

	以平均房价分类 By Average Room Rate				以主要市场分类 By Key Market				
	¥ 1,000 以上 Above ¥ 1,000	¥ 701~1,000 Between ¥ 701-1,000	¥ 401~700 Between ¥ 401-700	¥ 400 及以下 Below ¥ 400	北京 Beijing 五星/5-Star	上海 Shanghai 五星/5-Star	广州 Guangzhou 五星/5-Star	深圳 Shenzhen 五星/5-Star	三亚 Sanya 五星/5-Star
Labor Productivity									
Total Hotel Staff Per Available Room	**1.28**	**0.97**	**0.76**	**0.60**	**0.88**	**0.85**	**1.10**	**1.02**	**1.13**
Full Time	0.95	0.71	0.58	0.46	0.68	0.66	0.81	0.75	0.77
Part Time/Contract	0.18	0.14	0.09	0.09	0.14	0.12	0.15	0.14	0.14
Intern	0.15	0.12	0.08	0.05	0.07	0.07	0.14	0.12	0.21
Total Hotel Staff Per Occupied Room	**3.28**	**2.34**	**1.73**	**1.37**	**2.73**	**2.04**	**2.27**	**2.33**	**2.46**
Full Time	2.43	1.72	1.33	1.05	2.09	1.58	1.67	1.74	1.67
Part Time/Contract	0.47	0.33	0.21	0.20	0.44	0.28	0.30	0.31	0.32
Intern	0.39	0.28	0.19	0.12	0.21	0.17	0.30	0.27	0.47
Staff Hour Per Occupied Room - Rooms	**5.10**	**3.57**	**2.78**	**2.35**	**4.03**	**2.99**	**3.36**	**3.62**	**4.33**
Full Time	3.38	2.40	1.96	1.69	2.77	2.13	2.29	2.38	2.52
Part Time/Contract	1.11	0.74	0.53	0.45	0.88	0.59	0.64	0.81	1.08
Intern	0.61	0.42	0.29	0.20	0.38	0.28	0.43	0.43	0.74
Staff Hour Per Occupied Room - Total	**17.99**	**12.80**	**9.48**	**7.51**	**14.96**	**11.18**	**12.42**	**12.75**	**13.46**
Full Time	13.32	9.43	7.30	5.75	11.44	8.67	9.13	9.55	9.17
Part Time/Contract	2.55	1.82	1.15	1.11	2.39	1.56	1.66	1.71	1.73
Intern	2.13	1.55	1.03	0.64	1.12	0.96	1.63	1.50	2.56
Total F&B Staff Per Seat	**0.23**	**0.20**	**0.17**	**0.13**	**0.20**	**0.19**	**0.24**	**0.21**	**0.20**
Full Time	0.17	0.14	0.13	0.10	0.15	0.14	0.17	0.16	0.12
Part Time/Contract	0.02	0.01	0.01	0.01	0.02	0.02	0.02	0.01	0.01
Intern	0.05	0.04	0.03	0.02	0.03	0.03	0.05	0.04	0.07
Staff Hour Per Cover - F&B Total	**2.10**	**1.89**	**1.42**	**1.08**	**2.26**	**2.00**	**1.83**	**1.79**	**1.71**
Full Time	1.42	1.24	0.96	0.71	1.56	1.42	1.20	1.25	1.04
Part Time/Contract	0.32	0.32	0.21	0.21	0.44	0.34	0.28	0.25	0.16
Intern	0.37	0.34	0.25	0.16	0.26	0.25	0.35	0.29	0.51
Staff Hour Per Cover - Banquet	**3.09**	**2.60**	**1.67**	**1.67**	**4.70**	**2.75**	**1.91**	**2.59**	**4.05**
Full Time	1.61	1.18	0.83	0.80	2.32	1.57	0.92	1.21	1.92
Part Time/Contract	1.15	1.14	0.63	0.61	1.72	0.87	0.78	1.06	1.26
Intern	0.33	0.28	0.21	0.26	0.67	0.32	0.20	0.32	0.87

平均工资水平 – 管理阶层（按管理模式分类 – 五星级酒店）
Average Salary Scale - Supervisory Positions (By Management Model - 5-Star)

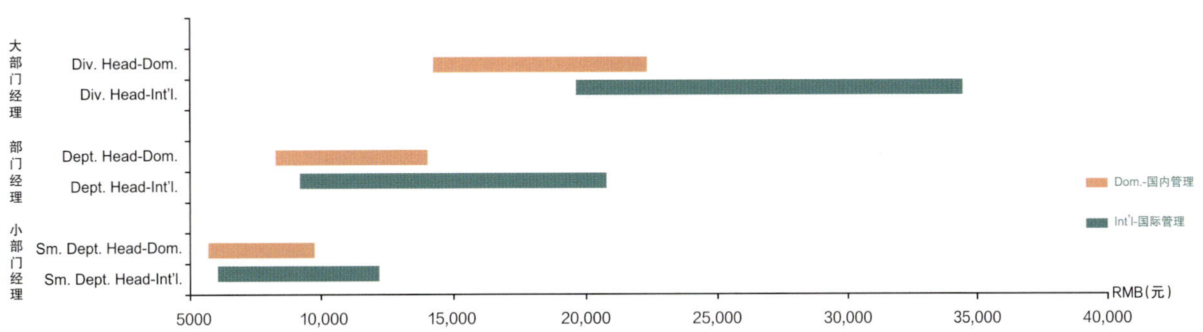

表 10　主要市场分类信息
TABLE 10　DISTRIBUTION OF HOTELS BY KEY MARKETS

		以地理区域划分 By Region						
		华北 North	东北 North East	华东 East	中南 South Central	西北 North West	西南 South West	合计 Total
样本酒店	**Category**							
以平均房价分类	**By Average Room Rate**							
样本酒店数量（家）	**No. of Hotels**							
1,000元以上	Above RMB 1,000	24	7	54	52	1	21	**159**
701~1,000元	Between RMB 701-1,000	33	7	60	37	4	28	**169**
401~700元	Between RMB 401-700	80	26	269	153	4	86	**618**
400元及以下	Below RMB 400	55	27	261	122	10	84	**559**
合计	**Total**	**192**	**67**	**644**	**364**	**19**	**219**	**1505**
所占比例	**Percentage Share**							
1,000元以上	Above RMB 1,000	13%	10%	8%	14%	5%	10%	**11%**
701~1,000元	Between RMB 701-1,000	17%	10%	9%	10%	21%	13%	**11%**
401~700元	Between RMB 401-700	42%	39%	42%	42%	21%	39%	**41%**
400元及以下	Below RMB 400	29%	40%	41%	34%	53%	38%	**37%**
合计	**Total**	**100%**	**100%**	**100%**	**100%**	**100%**	**100%**	**100%**
以星级分类	**By Star Rating**							
样本酒店数量（家）	**No. of Hotels**							
五星级	5-Star	110	44	429	233	14	146	**976**
四星级	4-Star	54	9	162	91	2	49	**367**
三星级+有限服务型	3-Star+Limited Service	28	14	53	40	3	24	**162**
合计	**Total**	**192**	**67**	**644**	**364**	**19**	**219**	**1505**
所占比例	**Percentage Share**							
五星级	5-Star	57%	66%	67%	64%	74%	67%	**65%**
四星级	4-Star	28%	13%	25%	25%	11%	22%	**24%**
三星级+有限服务型	3-Star+Limited Service	15%	21%	8%	11%	16%	11%	**11%**
合计	**Total**	**100%**	**100%**	**100%**	**100%**	**100%**	**100%**	**100%**
以管理模式分类	**By Management Model**							
样本酒店数量（家）	**No. of Hotels**							
国际管理五星级	International 5-Star	75	31	282	174	7	104	**673**
国内管理五星级	Domestic 5-Star	33	13	145	57	6	36	**290**
国际管理四星级	International 4-Star	28	6	78	47	1	29	**189**
国内管理四星级	Domestic 4-Star	26	3	79	41	1	15	**165**
合计	**Total**	**162**	**53**	**584**	**319**	**15**	**184**	**1317**
所占比例	**Percentage Share**							
国际管理五星级	International 5-Star	46%	58%	48%	55%	47%	57%	**51%**
国内管理五星级	Domestic 5-Star	20%	25%	25%	18%	40%	20%	**22%**
国际管理四星级	International 4-Star	17%	11%	13%	15%	7%	16%	**14%**
国内管理四星级	Domestic 4-Star	16%	6%	14%	13%	7%	8%	**13%**
合计	**Total**	**100%**	**100%**	**100%**	**100%**	**100%**	**100%**	**100%**

备注 Notes:

1. 各城市所占百分比的计算基于所有参与统计的酒店的有效数据。
   Distribution percentages are based on total usable responses collected for each category.

表 11 客房类型
TABLE 11 GUESTROOM STATISTICS

		以星级分类 By Star Rating			以管理模式分类 By Management Model			
		五星 5-Star	四星 4-Star	三星+有限服务 3-Star + Limited Service	国际管理 Int'l 五星/5-Star	国内管理 Dom. 五星/5-Star	国际管理 Int'l 四星/4-Star	国内管理 Dom. 四星/4-Star
客房	**Guestroom**							
客房类型数量（间）	**Room Mix Count**							
标准房	Standard	235	197	168	231	246	208	186
行政房	Executive	47	33	16	50	43	36	31
套房	Suite	35	24	7	37	31	28	20
别墅	Villa	3	1	0	3	3	0	1
合计	**Total**	**321**	**254**	**191**	**320**	**322**	**273**	**238**
所占比例	**Room Mix (%)**							
标准房	Standard	73%	77%	88%	72%	76%	76%	78%
行政房	Executive	15%	13%	8%	16%	13%	13%	13%
套房	Suite	11%	9%	4%	11%	9%	10%	9%
别墅	Villa	1%	0%	0%	1%	1%	0%	0%
合计	**Total**	**100%**	**100%**	**100%**	**100%**	**100%**	**100%**	**100%**
客房面积（平方米）	**Size Per Available Room (SQM)**							
标准房	Standard	43	35	30	44	40	37	34
行政房	Executive	47	38	36	47	46	38	39
套房	Suite	86	67	54	89	79	67	65
别墅	Villa	259	94	0	277	232	78	73
平均	**Average**	**50**	**39**	**31**	**52**	**47**	**40**	**37**

备注 Notes:

1. 客房面积为净面积，包括卫生间。
   Room size given is on a net basis and includes the bathroom.

图1　样本酒店构成信息
GRAPH 1　BREAKDOWN OF SURVEY RESPONSES

五星级酒店市场样本酒店数量–按管理模式划分

No. of 5-Star Responses by Management Model

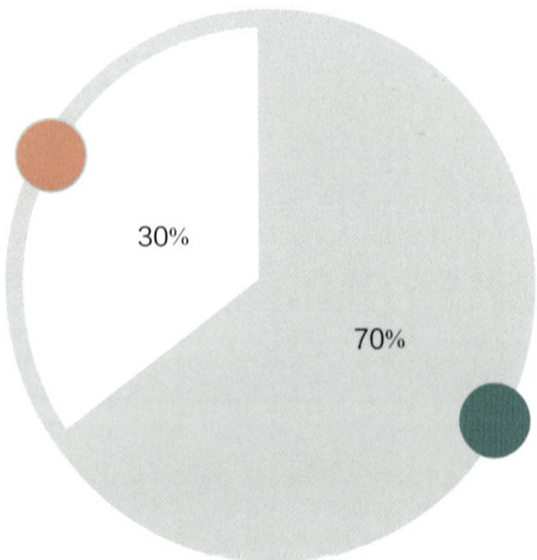

国际管理 673 家
International 673 Hotels

国内管理 290 家
Domestic 290 Hotels

四星级酒店市场样本酒店数量–按管理模式划分

No. of 4-Star Responses by Management Model

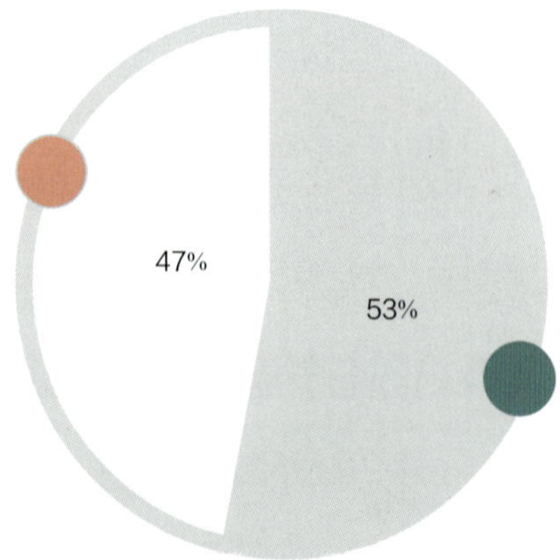

国际管理 189 家
International 189 Hotels

国内管理 165 家
Domestic 165 Hotels

样本酒店数量–按星级划分

No. of Responses by Star Rating

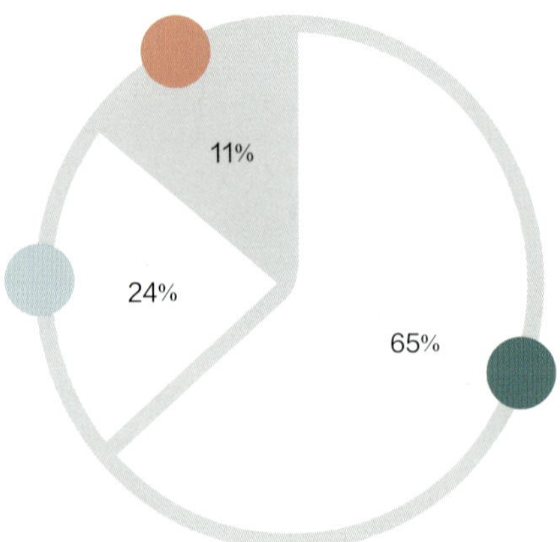

五星级酒店 976 家
5-Star 976 Hotels

四星级酒店 367 家
4-Star 367 Hotels

三星级+有限服务型酒店 162 家
3-Star + Limited Service 162 Hotels

样本酒店数量–按平均房价划分

No. of Responses by ADR Category

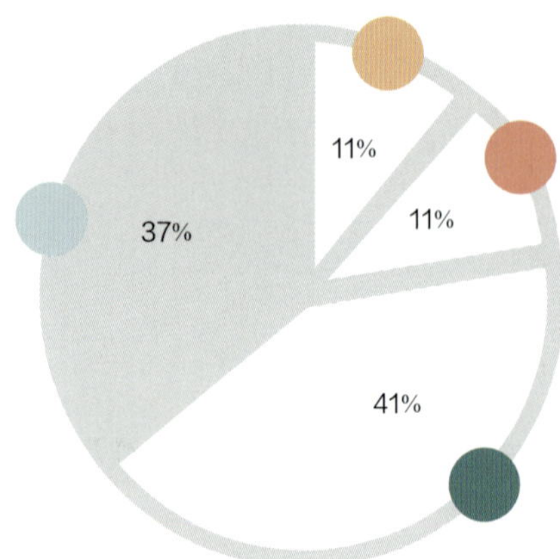

1,000元以上 159 家
Above RMB1,000, 159 Hotels

701~1,000元 169 家
RMB701-1,000, 169 Hotels

401~700元 618 家
RMB401-700, 618 Hotels

400元及以下 559 家
Below RMB400, 559 Hotels

图2 客源构成及房价贡献
GRAPH 2 MARKET MIX & ADR CONTRIBUTION

五星级市场 客源构成及房价贡献（元）
5-Star Hotels Market Mix & ADR Contribution (RMB)

- 散客－商务散客 577 Transient - Corporate/Business FIT
- 散客－直接散客 855 Transient - Direct FIT
- 散客－批发/包价散客 855 Transient - Wholesale/Package FIT
- 团队－酒店内会议团队 492 Group - In-House Meeting
- 团队－会议/会展/奖励旅游 540 Group - Other MICE
- 团队－旅游团队 519 Group - Leisure Group
- 无预订散客 784 Other - Walk-in
- 政府客源 382 Other - Government
- 航空机组人员 456 Other - Airline
- 其他 591 Other

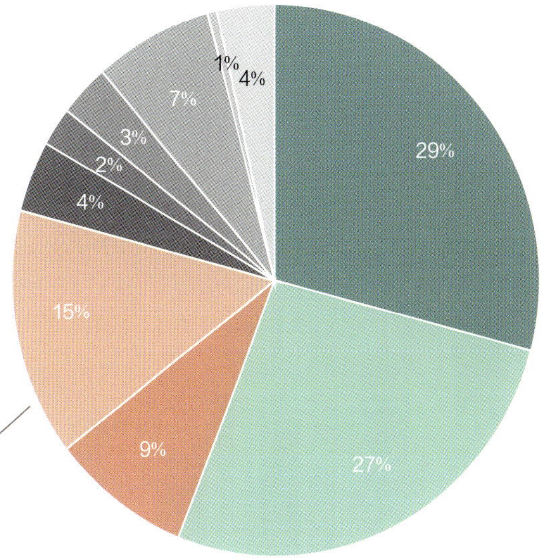

四星级市场 客源构成及房价贡献（元）
4-Star Hotels Market Mix & ADR Contribution (RMB)

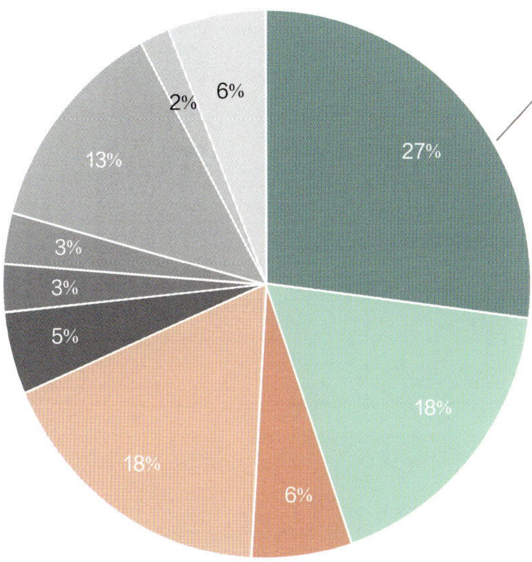

- 散客－商务散客 397 Transient - Corporate/Business FIT
- 散客－直接散客 463 Transient - Direct FIT
- 散客－批发/包价散客 451 Transient - Wholesale/Package FIT
- 团队－酒店内会议团队 347 Group - In-House Meeting
- 团队－会议/会展/奖励旅游 367 Group - Other MICE
- 团队－旅游团队 341 Group - Leisure Group
- 无预订散客 467 Other - Walk-in
- 政府客源 351 Other - Government
- 航空机组人员 396 Other - Airline
- 其他 393 Other

- 散客－商务散客 347 Transient - Corporate/Business FIT
- 散客－直接散客 336 Transient - Direct FIT
- 散客－批发/包价散客 356 Transient - Wholesale/Package FIT
- 团队－酒店内会议团队 350 Group - In-House Meeting
- 团队－会议/会展/奖励旅游 341 Group - Other MICE
- 团队－旅游团队 318 Group - Leisure Group
- 无预订散客 319 Other - Walk-in
- 政府客源 284 Other - Government
- 航空机组人员 241 Other - Airline
- 其他 301 Other

三星级+有限服务型市场 客源构成及房价贡献（元）
3-Star+Limited Service Hotels Market Mix & ADR Contribution (RMB)

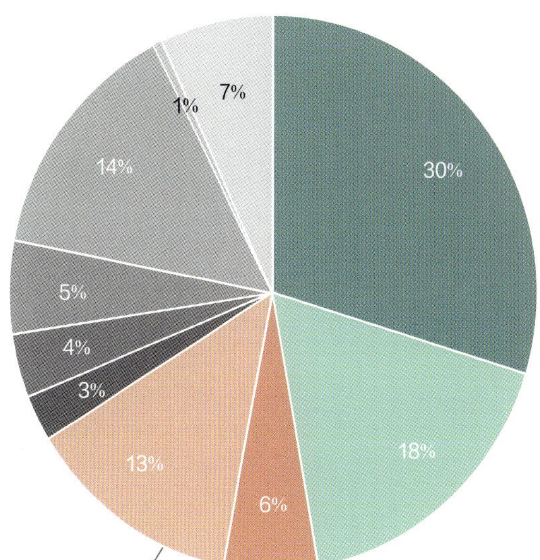

图3 部分城市业绩指标比较
GRAPH 3 KEY CITIES PERFORMANCE INDICATORS

图4 收入及支出构成
GRAPH 4 PERCENTAGE OF DISTRIBUTION OF REVENUES AND EXPENSES

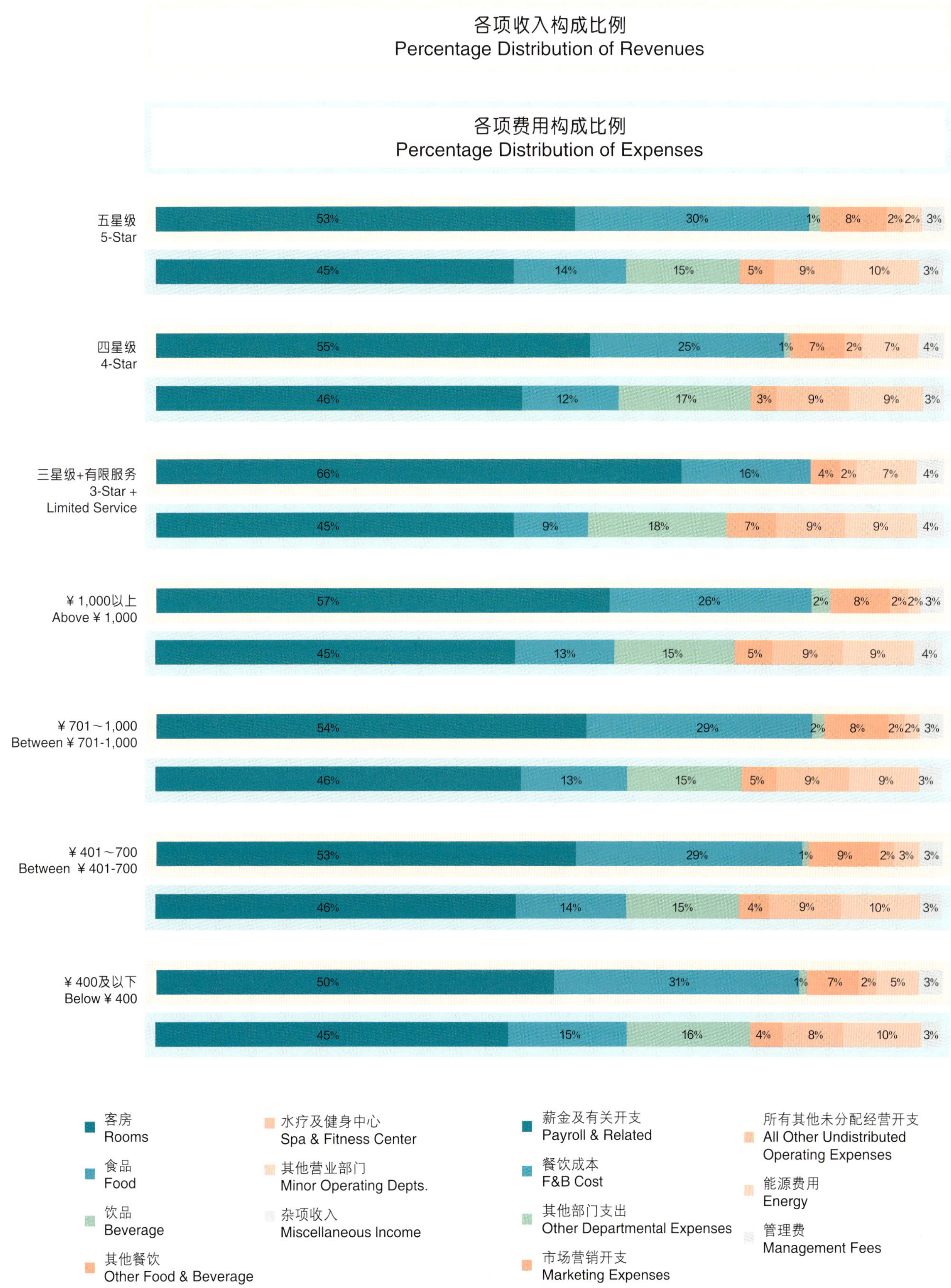

图5　酒店历史业绩比较

酒店基本业绩指标比较（按星级划分），2018~2022年
General Performance Comparison (By Star Rating), 2018-2022

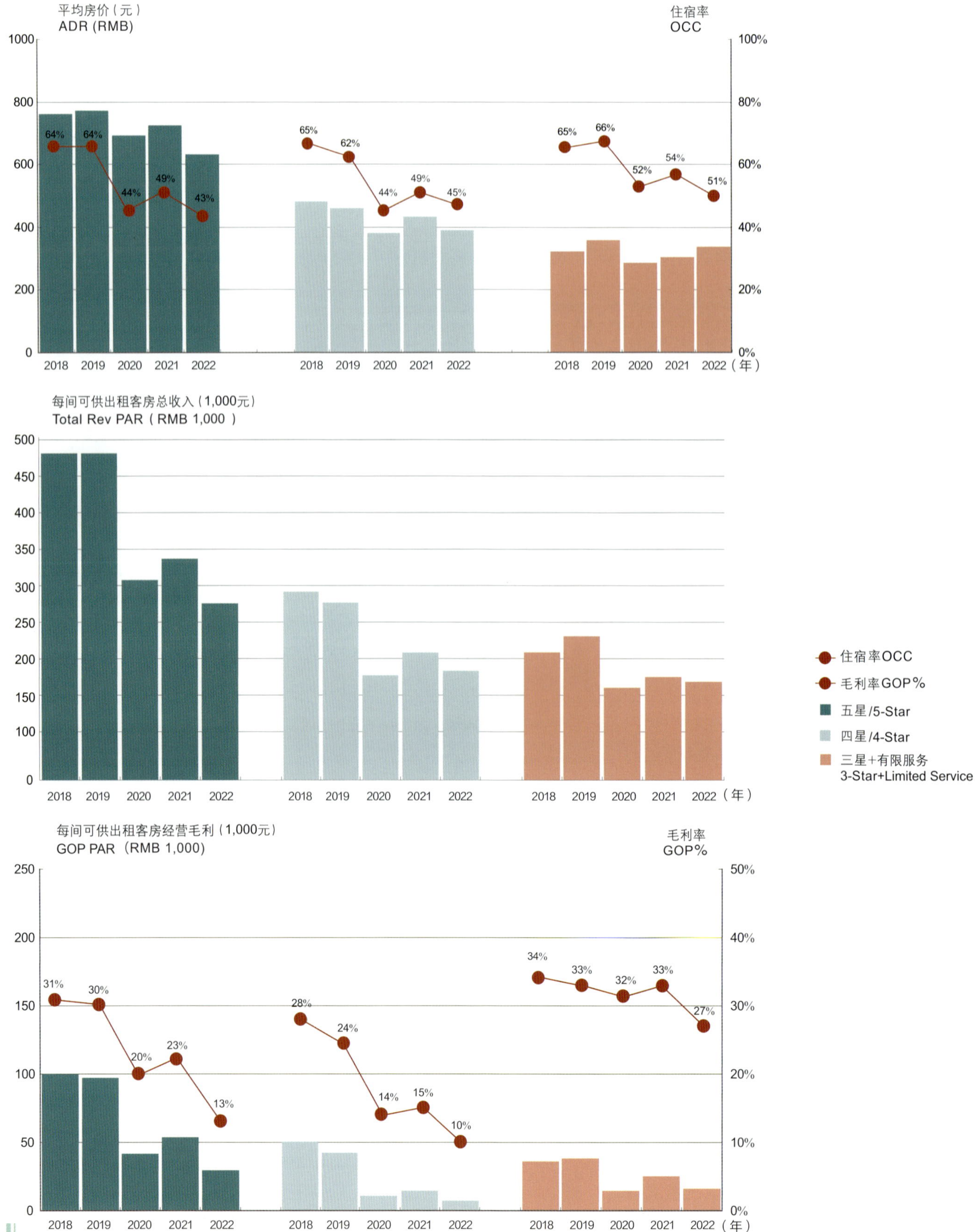

酒店基本业绩指标比较（按管理模式划分），2018~2022
General Performance Comparison（By Management Model），2018-2022

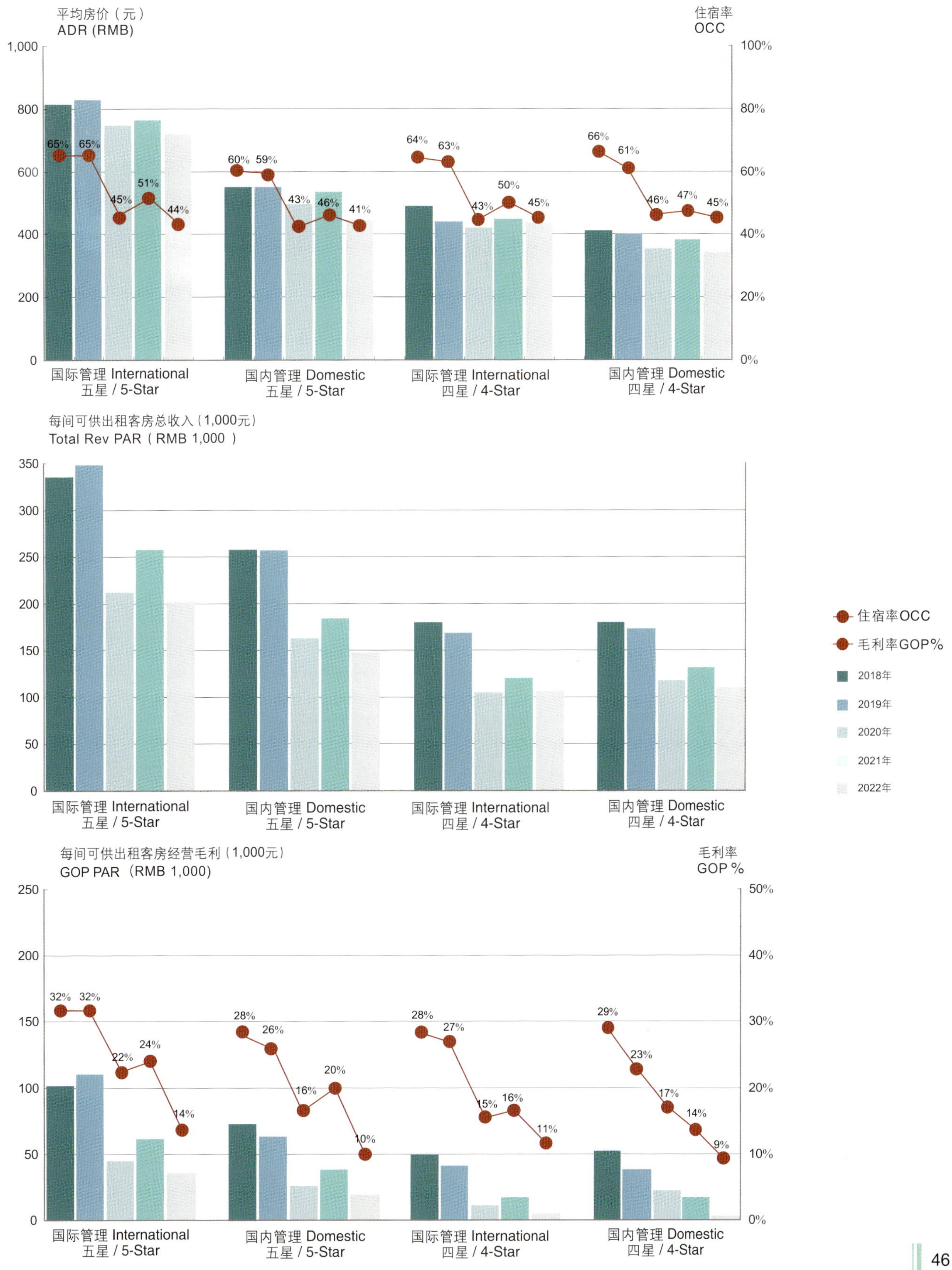

图6　酒店业绩景气预测
GRAPH 6　PERFORMANCE FORECAST

预测2023年住宿率及平均房价“上升”的酒店所占比例
2023 Occupancy & Average Rate Forecast - % Answered “Improve”

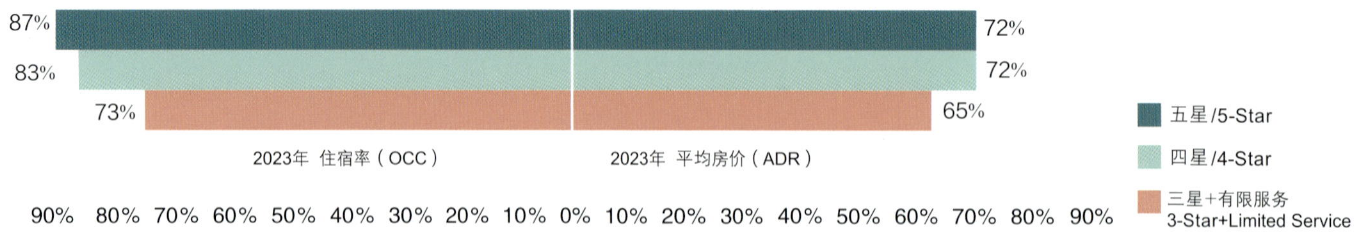

2022年(实际)与2023年(预测)住宿率比较
2022 (Actual) and 2023 (Forecast) Occupancy Comparison

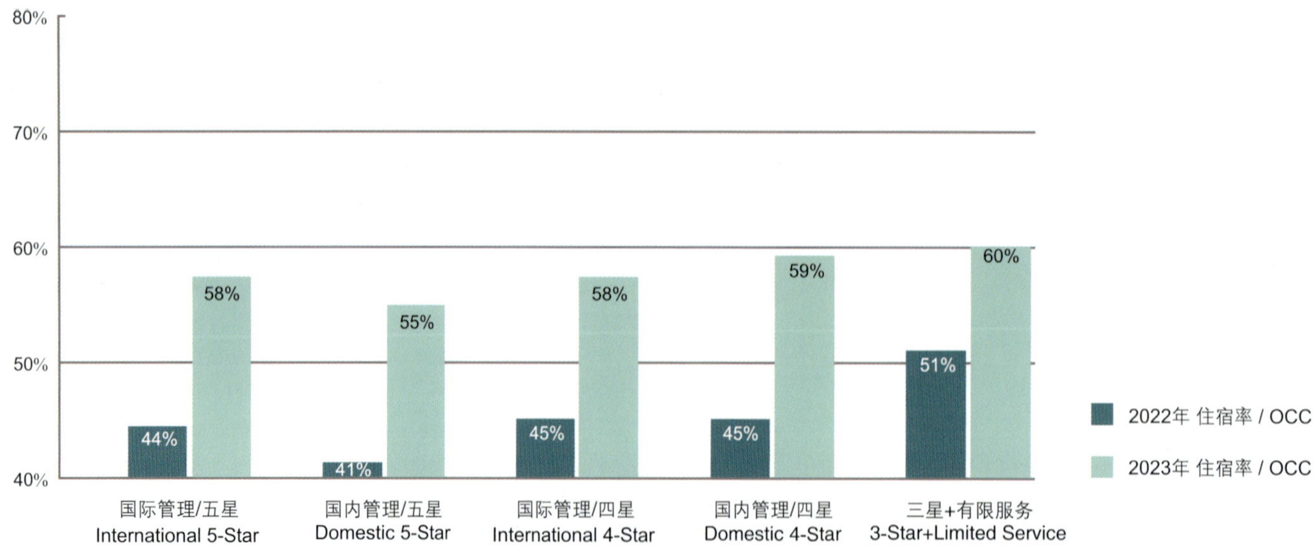

2022年(实际)与2023年(预测)平均房价比较
2022 (Actual) and 2023 (Forecast) Average Rate Comparison

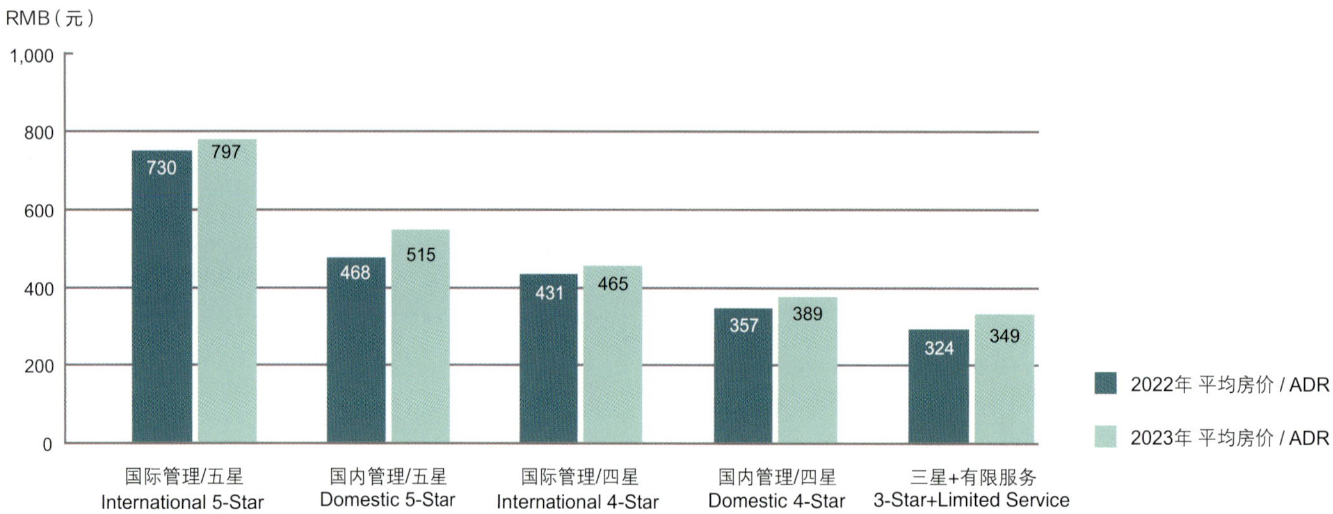

附录一 中国旅游饭店业协会简介
APPENDIX 1 ABOUT CHINA TOURIST HOTEL ASSOCIATION

中国旅游饭店业协会，英文名称为China Tourist Hotel Association（英文缩写：CTHA），成立于1986年2月，经中华人民共和国民政部登记注册，具有独立的法人资格。

中国旅游饭店业协会是由中国境内的旅游饭店和地方饭店协会、饭店管理公司、饭店信息系统供应和服务商、饭店线上运营商、饭店院校、饭店用品供应厂商等相关单位和饭店专家及资深学者自愿结成的行业性的全国性的非营利性的社会组织。

中国旅游饭店业协会的宗旨：遵守国家的宪法、法律、法规和有关政策，遵守社会道德风尚，代表和维护中国旅游饭店行业的共同利益，维护会员的合法权益，在登记管理机关、党建领导机关和行业管理部门的业务指导和监督管理下，为会员服务，为行业服务，在政府与会员之间发挥桥梁和纽带作用，为促进我国旅游饭店业的健康发展做出积极贡献。

中国旅游饭店业协会为会员服务范围：宣传、贯彻国家有关旅游业的发展方针和旅游饭店行业的政策、法规；向业务主管单位反映会员的愿望和要求；组织会员订立行规行约并监督遵守，维护旅游饭店的市场秩序；开展饭店业的调查研究，协助饭店业务主管单位搞好行业管理；交流旅游饭店的工作经验，收集国内外饭店业的信息；接受政府有关部门委托或根据市场和行业发展需要，组织开展饭店的培训、研讨、考察及有关产品展览等工作；对相关标准参与实施，开展认证等工作；领导下设的专业委员会开展业务活动；开展和国际饭店与住宿业协会等相关行业组织之间的交流与合作。

中国旅游饭店业协会会员中聚集了全国饭店行业中知名度高、影响力大、服务规范、信誉良好的星级饭店，以及国内外有影响力的饭店集团和知名饭店品牌。

目前，中国旅游饭店业协会共有会员1461家，理事单位 386家，常务理事49人，副会长22人，秘书长1人。李峰先生为协会现任会长。

中国旅游饭店业协会于1994年正式加入国际饭店与餐馆协会（英文缩写为IH&RA）。

自2009年6月起，中国旅游饭店业协会秘书处承担全国旅游星级饭店评定委员会办公室职能。

副会长（按姓氏笔画排列）：凡东升、王　志、王　健、王建平、王海军、仲　勇、刘凯强、孙　坚、孙　健、孙子元、狄　嘉、张　添、张晓强、陆　洋、陈瑞亮、金　辉、陈　蓉、钱　利、郭　庆、梁晓京、颜雪巍、戴雪英

Registered at the Ministry of Civil Affairs of the People's Republic of China, China Tourist Hotel Association ("CTHA") was established in February 1986 as an independent legal entity. CTHA is a national non-profit industry organization formed, in a voluntary manner, by the Association of Tourist Hotels and Local Hotels, hotel management companies, manufacturer of hotel information systems, online hotel operators, hotel academies, hotel equipment & supplies providers and other relevant organizations in the territory of China as well as the hotel experts and senior scholars.

Tenet of CTHA: to abide by the constitution, laws, regulations and relevant policies, comply with the social moralities, represent and protect the common interests of Chinese tourist hotel industry and the legal rights and interests of members of CTHA, registration authority, party building leading authority, build a bridge and link between the members and the governments and make a positive contribution to the healthy development of Chinese tourist hotel industry.

Scope of services for CTHA Members: publicity and implementation of national development guidelines related to the tourism industry and the policies and regulations on the tourist hotel industry; reporting the aspirations and requirements of the members to the competent authorities; organizing the members to develop the industry rules and regulations and supervising their compliance to maintain the market order of tourist hotels; carrying out the investigations and studies on the hotel industry and assisting the competent authorities of hotels in the industry management; exchanging the working experience of tourist hotels and collecting information of the hotel industries both at home and abroad; based on the entrustment of relevant governmental authorities or according to the requirements for market and industry development, organizing and conducting the hotel-targeted training, discussions, visits and relevant product exhibitions; participating in the implementation of relevant standards and carrying out the certification work; leading the operational activities of its special committees; conducting the exchanges and cooperation with international hotel & lodging associations and other relevant industry organizations.

CTHA has gathered a lot of star-rated hotels with great fame, wide influence, standard service and high reputation, as well as influential worldwide hotel groups and famous hotel brands. Up to now, there have been 1461 members, 386 directors, 49 standing directors, 22 Deputy Chairman and a secretary general in CTHA. Mr. Li Feng is the Chairman of the association.

In the year of 1994, CTHA was recruited into International Hotel & Restaurant Association (Abb. As IH&RA).

Since June 2009, The CTHA Secretariat has undertook the functions of China Tourist Hotel Star-Rating Committee Office.

Deputy Chairman: Fan Dongsheng, Wang Zhi, Wang Jian, Wang Jianping, Wang Haijun, Zhong Yong, Liu Kaiqiang, Sun Jian, Sun Jian, Sun Ziyuan, Di Jia, Zhang Tian, Zhang Xiaoqiang, Lu Yang, Chen Ruiliang, Jin Hui, Chen Rong, Qian Li, Guo Qing, Liang Xiaojing, Yan Xuewei, Dai Xueying.

作为一个拥有百年历史的专业咨询品牌，浩华，参与了20世纪五十年代《全球酒店业统一会计准则》的创立，并于2003年正式在北京开设中国大陆地区的第一间办公室。浩华与中国旅游饭店业协会通力合作，自2003年开始，每年度正式出版的《中国饭店业务统计》现已成为行业业务标杆数据发布和分享的权威专业刊物。浩华致力于以前瞻性视角引领行业趋势和推动行业变革，率先在业内推出〝空间坪效〞概念，以推动行业精准化投资、空间功能规划及持续优化的资产管理举措，并首创了市场景气指数（MSI）及市场价值指数（MVI）两大指数体系。2022年，浩华正式推出“厚海数据平台”，进一步构建酒旅行业专业的数据标准和评价体系，参与推动行业数字化转型和全面效能提升。浩华深耕中国市场超过二十年，在超过280个城市和目的地，累计完成了超过2000个顾问咨询项目，积累了丰富的项目咨询经验。迈入新周期，依托“浩华”“厚海”及“CHAT”三大业务品牌，浩华将覆盖企业发展、目的地及住宿产业的全生命周期业务矩阵，为我们的客户提供从宏观到微观、从战略到落地的专业解决方案。以数据精神、破立自新、长期主义为核心价值观，浩华将以“致力于推动美好生活方式产业持续进化”作为企业发展愿景。

多维度及全生命周期专业解决方案

三大品牌及业务板块

APPENDIX 2 ABOUT HORWATH HTL

Horwath HTL (hereinafter referred to as HHTL), a professional consulting brand with a century-long history, participated in the establishment of the *Uniform Systems of Accounts for Hotels* in the 1950s. In 2003, it officially opened its first office in Beijing in Mainland China. Since 2003, HHTL has collaborated with the China Tourist Hotel Association and jointly published the *China Hotel Industry Study*, which has become an authoritative professional publication for industry benchmarking data. HHTL is committed to leading industry trends and advocating industry reforms from a forward-thinking perspective. It first introduced the concept of "space efficiency" in the industry to promote proper investment, space function planning, and continuous asset management optimization. Meanwhile, it also created two significant index systems, MSI (Market Sentiment Index) and MVI (Market Value Index). In 2022, Horwath HTL officially launched the "HOHI Data Platform" to further build the professional standard and evaluation system for the data of the hotel and tourism industry, while also promoting industry digital transformation and efficiency improvement. HHTL has consulted on more than 2,000 projects in about 280 cities and destinations throughout China over the past 20 years, accumulating extensive project consulting experience. In the new cycle, HHTL will rely on its three primary business brands — Horwath, HOHI, and CHAT to cover the entire life cycle business matrix of the destination and lodging industry, providing professional solutions from macro to micro, from strategy to implementation for clients. As HHTL's development vision, it will "strive to promote the continuous evolution of the good lifestyle industry" by leveraging the essential values of data spirit, innovation, and long-termism.

Multi-dimensional and Full Life Cycle Professional Solutions

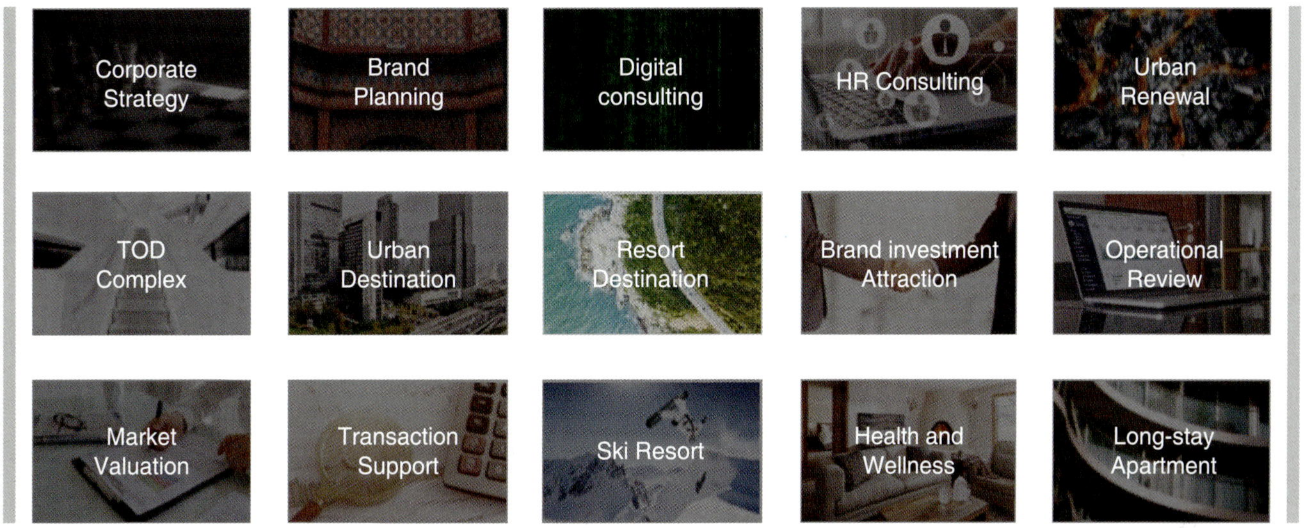

Three Major Brands and Business Segments

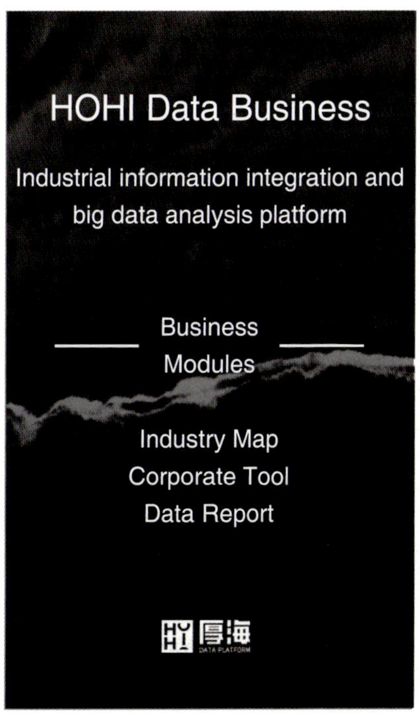

客房营业收入—本类别包括按半日、全日或更长时间出租客房所得的客房收入。该收入中包含服务费收入，但不包括将服务费用于酒店职工的工资或小费的部分，也不包括计入房费中的营业税。提供饮食、会议服务的公共场所/宴会厅、会议室、商务中心、房内饮品、洗衣等收入均不计入客房营业收入之内。

食品营业收入—本类别包括酒店餐厅、客房送餐、迷你吧、宴会和其他餐饮服务销售食品及非酒精饮品所得的收入。此项数据不含服务费和客人支付给餐厅服务员的小费。

饮品营业收入—本类别包括酒店向顾客销售所有酒精类饮品所得的收入。此项数据不含服务费和客人支付给餐厅服务员的小费。

其他餐饮收入—本类别包括了视听设备租赁、公共场所租赁所得收入、服务费和各色其他收入。该收入中包含餐饮部门的服务费。

其他营运部门营业收入—本类别包括客衣洗涤和干洗及停车场等其他小型营运部门所产生的收入。

杂项收入—本类别包括与第三方相关的收入或不会招致任何直接营运费用的收入。如：外币兑换产生的利润或损失、商业场地租金和使用权出让费、佣金、顾客取消预订收取的罚金及现金折扣等。

食品营业成本—本类别包括为客人提供食品及非酒精饮品所需成本。此数字按实际记账金额计算。酒店职工膳食成本（在所属部门记账）不构成售出食品成本的一部分。

饮品营业成本—本类别指各种酒精类饮品的成本。此数字按实际记账金额计算，酒店职工饮品成本（在所属部门记账）不构成售出饮品成本的一部分。

其他营运部门销售成本—包括客衣洗涤和干洗、停车场和任何其他小型营运部门所产生的销售成本。

客房部工资及有关开支—本类别包括付给客房部人员（前厅、楼层、布草管理及调配、预订、行李生、门童等）的薪金；其他福利开支包括社会保险、医疗津贴、教育津贴、房屋津贴、有薪假期等员工福利，免费或按明显优惠价提供给职工的货品及服务，以及职工膳食、奖励、社交活动及退休金（若适用）。

餐饮部工资及有关开支—本类别包括付给餐饮部人员（采购、收货、储存、备餐、服务、餐具洁净、收银及监督人员）的薪金；其他福利开支包括社会保险、医疗津贴、教育津贴、房屋津贴、有薪假期等员工福利，免费或按明显优惠价提供给职工的货品及服务，以及职工膳食、奖励、社交活动及退休金（若适用）。

其他营运部门工资及有关开支—本类别包含所有其他营运部门员工的薪水、工资、奖金和相关人工费用。其他营运部门相关人工费用包括工资税、补助性工资（如：假期工资、节日工资、病假工资、搬家费用、带薪假期和解雇费等），以及员工福利支出（如：由雇主支付的健康保险费用、养老金、员工膳食成本等）等。

其他开支—其他开支一词可能会引起混淆。乍眼看来，这词无严格释义，如工资及其他开支可解释为工资及营运某项设施所引起之所有额外开支。其实，本词有精确意义，意指营运有关部门所引起的直接部门开支。

客房部其他开支—本类别指不属于客房部工资（按上段定义）的其他开支，如有线/卫星电视、清洁物资、布草、佣金、免费赠送服务和礼品、客用物资、打印设备和文具、常客费用、设备租赁、总部人员住宿补偿等方面的费用。

餐饮部其他开支—本类别包括餐饮部门的非人工支出，包括：瓷器、玻璃器具、清洁用品、装饰品、客房用品、洗熨、织物、音乐及娱乐、菜单及饮品类目录、银器、制服等。

其他营运部门其他开支—本类别包括所有其他营运部门的非人工支出，包括：电话设备租赁、洗涤物资供应等方面的费用。

未分配经营开支—本类别用于：(1) 行政及一般开支；(2) 信息与通信系统开支；(3) 市场及营销开支；(4) 能源成本；(5) 物业营运及保养费。此五项中每一项均可视为一单项。这些开支内容可包括：

行政及一般开支 - 包含行政及后勤部门员工的薪水、工资、奖金和相关人工费用，及此部门的非人工费用，如：银行手续费、商务办公开支、信用卡手续费、法律顾问费用、经营物资供应、顾问费以及许可证照费等。
信息与通信系统开支 - 包含信息与通信部门的员工薪水、工资、奖金和相关人工费用，及此部门的非人工费用，如：互联网费用、通信费用、系统费用（包括软件许可与维护费、软件服务费、存储费、技术支持费等）。
市场及营销开支 - 包含销售和市场推广部门员工的薪水、工资、奖金和相关人工费用，及此部门的非人工费用，如：广告、销售、促销、商品推广、公关和市场调研所发生的支出、以及适当的差旅与招待费用及物资支出等。
能源成本 - 包含电力、煤气、燃料、蒸汽、用水等方面的开支和公共事业税等。
物业营运及保养费 - 包含物业营运及维保部门员工的薪水、工资、奖金和相关人工费用，及此部门的非人工费用，如：维修建筑、机电设备、地板、家具和运营设施、地面和景观照明灯泡、其他机械产品和垃圾清运等发生的成本。

非经营相关收入及支出前收益— 在本研究中，非经营相关收入及支出前收益指的是经营毛利减去酒店总管理费用的余额。

Room Revenue - This category includes revenue from guest accommodation rented on a part-day, full-day, or longer period basis. The figures include service charges but exclude hotel accommodation tax and tips given to employees. Revenue from public/function rooms ordinarily used for food and beverage service is not included in room sales.

Food Revenue - This category includes revenue derived from the sale of food and non-alcoholic beverages from restaurants, in-room dining, mini bar, banquets, or catering. The figures exclude service charges and tips given to employees.

Beverage Revenue - This category includes revenue from the sale of alcoholic beverages for consumption by customers. The figures exclude service charges and tips given to employees.

Other Food and Beverage Revenue - This category includes revenues generated from audiovisual equipment rentals, public room rentals, service charges and miscellaneous other revenue. The figures include service charges for the food and beverage department.

Other Operated Departments Revenue - This category includes revenue derived from laundry and dry cleaning, parking garage, etc.

Miscellaneous Income - Revenues related to a third party or revenues that do not incur any direct operating expenses, including foreign currency transaction gains (losses), space, rentals and concessions, commissions, cancelation penalties, cash discounted earned, etc.

Cost of Food Sales -This category includes the cost of food (and non-alcoholic beverages) served to guests in all segments of food revenues.

Cost of Beverage Sales -This category includes the cost of alcoholic beverages served to guests in all segments of beverage revenues.

Cost of Other Operated Departments Sales- This category represents the sales cost derived from laundry and dry cleaning, parking garage and any other minor operated departments.

Rooms Payroll & Related Expenses - This category includes salaries, wages plus service charge percentage (if applicable) paid to personnel of the rooms department (front office, maids, doormen and porters). Also included are the employee benefits such as social insurance, medical allowance, education, housing allowance, vacation and holiday pay, goods and services to employees free of charge or at markedly reduced prices, employees' meals, awards, social activities and pensions, if any.

Food and Beverage Payroll & Related Expenses - This category includes salaries, wages plus service charge percentage (if applicable) paid to personnel in the food and beverage department (purchasing, receiving, storage, preparation, service, dishwashing, cashiers and control). Also included are the employee benefits such as social insurance, medical allowance, education, housing allowance, vacation and holiday pay, goods and services to employees free of charge or at markedly reduced prices, employees' meals, awards, social activities and pensions, if any.

Other Operated Departments Payroll & Related Expenses - This category includes the expenses associated with salaries, wages and bonuses and payroll-related expenses for employees in all other departments. Payroll-related expenses include payroll taxes, supplemental pay (such as vacation pay, holiday pay, sick pay, relocation pay, paid time off and severance pay), and employee benefits (such as employer-paid health insurance expenses, pension contributions, cost of meals furnished to employees, etc).

Other Expenses - The term "other expenses" can cause confusion. At first glance, it is a loose term - for example, the expression "wages and other expenses" could be interpreted as "wages and all additional expenses incurred in operating a facility". However, its meaning is precise and refers to direct departmental expenses incurred in the operation of a department or service (rooms department, sales office).

Rooms, Other Expenses - This category represents the non-payroll expenses for the room department, including the expenses of reservation expenses, travel agents' commissions, cable/satellite television, cleaning supplies, linen, commissions, complementary services and gifts, guest supplies, printing and stationery, royalty fees, equipment rentals, corporate office reimbursables, etc.

Food & Beverage, Other Expenses - This category includes the non-payroll expenses for the food and beverage department, including china and glassware, cleaning supplies, decorations, guest supplies, music and entertainment, silver and uniforms, etc.

Other Operated Departments, Other Expenses - This category includes the non-payroll expenses for all other operated departments, including telephone equipment rental, laundry supplies, etc.

Undistributed Operating Expenses - This classification is used for the following five expenses. Each of these can be considered as an individual entity. Some examples of the expenses included are:

Administrative & General expenses - Expenses comprise salaries, wages, bonuses and payroll-related expenses for employees as well as the non-payroll expenses such as cash overages or shortages, commissions on credit cards, collection charges, executive office expenses, general insurance, postal charges, legal expenses, trade association dues, travelling expenses, accountants' and consultants' fees.

Information & Telecommunications Systems expenses - Expenses comprise salaries, wages, bonuses and payroll-related expenses for employees as well as the non-payroll expenses such as cost of internet services, cost of calls, system expenses including software licenses and maintenance, software as service fees, hosting storage fees and technical support fees, etc.

Sales & Marketing expenses - Expenses comprise salaries, wages, bonuses and payroll-related expenses for employees as well as the non-payroll expenses such as advertising, sales, promotion, merchandising, public relations and research, plus applicable travel and entertainment expenses and supplies.

Energy costs - Include the cost of electrical power, fuel, steam, water,utility taxes,etc.

Property Operation & Maintenance expenses - Expenses comprise salaries, wages, bonuses and payroll-related expenses for employees as well as the non-payroll expenses such as the cost of repairing buildings, electrical and mechanical equipment and fixtures, floor coverings, furniture, grounds and landscaping plus the cost of electric bulbs, mechanical supplies and removal of waste matter.

Income Before Non-operating Income and Expenses - For the purposes of this study, Income Before Non-operating Income and Expenses is calculated by subtracting total management fees from gross operating profit.

酒店业绩对照自测表

PROPERTY BENCHMARKING WORKSHEET

每日可供出租客房 (A):______________

全年实际入住客房 (B):______________

		2022年 业绩 2022 Performance (C)	每一可供 出租客房 Per Available Room (C/A)	每一实际 入住客房 Per Occupied Room (C/B)	占收入 百分比 % of Revenue
部门收入	**Departmental Revenues**				
客房	Rooms				
食品	Food				
饮品	Beverage				
其他餐饮	Other Food & Beverage				
水疗及健身	Spa & Fitness Center				
其他营运部门	Other Operated Depts.				
杂项收入	Miscellaneous Income				
合计	**Total**				
部门支出	**Departmental Expenses**				
客房	Rooms				
餐饮	Food & Beverage				
水疗及健身	Spa & Fitness Center				
其他营运部门	Other Operated Depts.				
杂项收入	Miscellaneous Income				
合计	**Total**				
部门盈利(亏损)	**Departmental Profit (Loss)**				
客房	Rooms				
餐饮	Food & Beverage				
水疗及健身	Spa & Fitness Center				
其他营运部门	Other Operated Depts.				
杂项收入	Miscellaneous Income				
合计	**Total**				
未分配经营开支	**Undistributed Operating Expenses**				
行政及一般开支	Administrative & General				
信息及通信系统	Information & Telecommunications				
市场推广及营销	Marketing				
能源	Energy				
物业营运及保养	Property Operation				
合计	**Total**				
经营毛利	**Gross Operating Profit**				
部门详细业绩	**Departmental Comparison**				
部门：__________	Dept.：______________				
部门直接成本	Direct Cost of Goods				
工资及相关开支	Payroll & Related Exp.				
其他开支	Other Expenses				
部门：__________	Dept.：______________				
部门直接成本	Direct Cost of Goods				
工资及相关开支	Payroll & Related Exp.				
其他开支	Other Expenses				
部门：__________	Dept.：______________				
部门直接成本	Direct Cost of Goods				
工资及相关开支	Payroll & Related Exp.				
其他开支	Other Expenses				
其他比较项目	**Other Line Item Comparison**				

每日可供出租客房：指平均每日所有客房扣除不可供出租的客房数（如装修、维修房等）。

全年实际入住客房：指实际占用的客房间夜数扣除免费馈赠房和总经理用房之后的已出售间夜总数。

饭店开发/改造的理想流程
IDEAL HOTEL DEVELOPMENT PROCESS

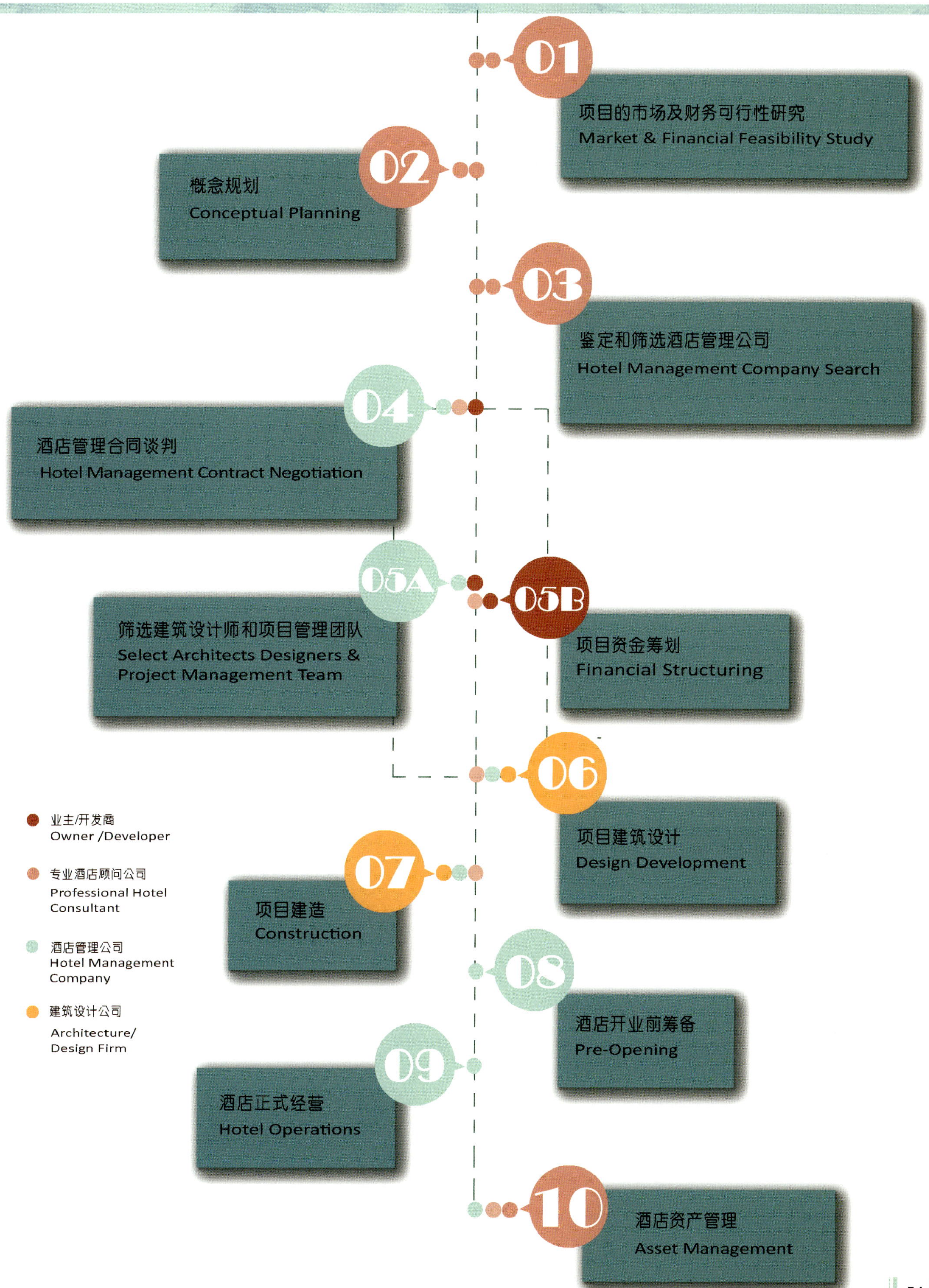

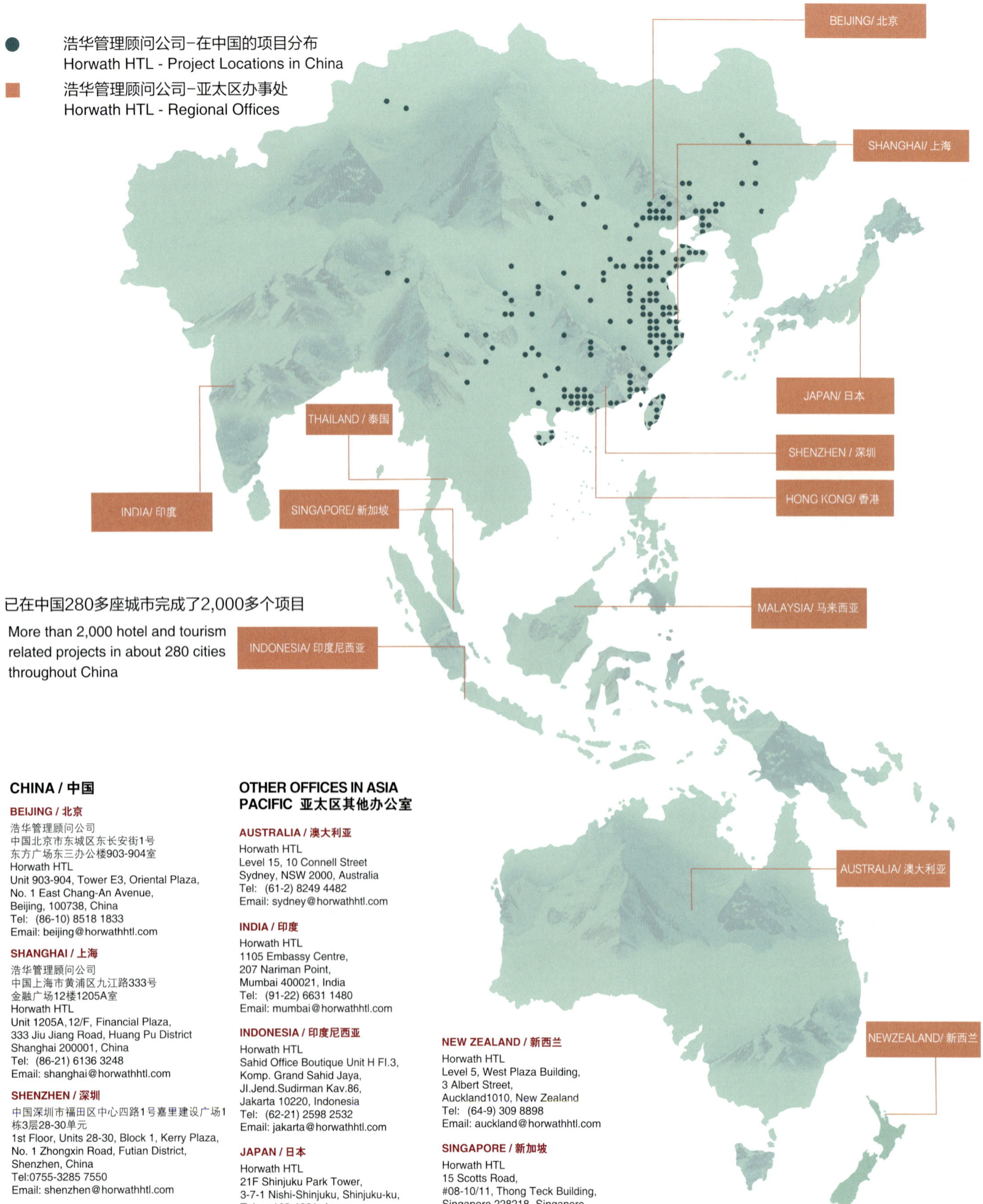

已在中国280多座城市完成了2,000多个项目

More than 2,000 hotel and tourism related projects in about 280 cities throughout China

CHINA / 中国

BEIJING / 北京

浩华管理顾问公司
中国北京市东城区东长安街1号
东方广场东三办公楼903-904室
Horwath HTL
Unit 903-904, Tower E3, Oriental Plaza,
No. 1 East Chang-An Avenue,
Beijing, 100738, China
Tel: (86-10) 8518 1833
Email: beijing@horwathhtl.com

SHANGHAI / 上海

浩华管理顾问公司
中国上海市黄浦区九江路333号
金融广场12楼1205A室
Horwath HTL
Unit 1205A, 12/F, Financial Plaza,
333 Jiu Jiang Road, Huang Pu District
Shanghai 200001, China
Tel: (86-21) 6136 3248
Email: shanghai@horwathhtl.com

SHENZHEN / 深圳

中国深圳市福田区中心四路1号嘉里建设广场1栋3层28-30单元
1st Floor, Units 28-30, Block 1, Kerry Plaza,
No. 1 Zhongxin Road, Futian District,
Shenzhen, China
Tel:0755-3285 7550
Email: shenzhen@horwathhtl.com

HONG KONG / 香港

浩华管理顾问公司
香港湾仔港湾道18号中环广场3807室
Horwath HTL
Suite 3807, 38/F Central Plaza
18 Harbour Road, Hong Kong
Tel: (852) 2524 6073
Email: hongkong@horwathhtl.com

OTHER OFFICES IN ASIA PACIFIC 亚太区其他办公室

AUSTRALIA / 澳大利亚

Horwath HTL
Level 15, 10 Connell Street
Sydney, NSW 2000, Australia
Tel: (61-2) 8249 4482
Email: sydney@horwathhtl.com

INDIA / 印度

Horwath HTL
1105 Embassy Centre,
207 Nariman Point,
Mumbai 400021, India
Tel: (91-22) 6631 1480
Email: mumbai@horwathhtl.com

INDONESIA / 印度尼西亚

Horwath HTL
Sahid Office Boutique Unit H Fl.3,
Komp. Grand Sahid Jaya,
Jl.Jend.Sudirman Kav.86,
Jakarta 10220, Indonesia
Tel: (62-21) 2598 2532
Email: jakarta@horwathhtl.com

JAPAN / 日本

Horwath HTL
21F Shinjuku Park Tower,
3-7-1 Nishi-Shinjuku, Shinjuku-ku,
Tokyo 163-1021, Japan
Tel: (81-3) 6911 2030
Email: tokyo@horwathhtl.com

MALAYSIA / 马来西亚

Horwath HTL
CEO Suite Level 36,
Menara Maxis, KLCC,
Kuala Lumpur, 50088, Malaysia
Tel: (60-3) 2615 0122
Email: kl@horwathhtl.com

NEW ZEALAND / 新西兰

Horwath HTL
Level 5, West Plaza Building,
3 Albert Street,
Auckland1010, New Zealand
Tel: (64-9) 309 8898
Email: auckland@horwathhtl.com

SINGAPORE / 新加坡

Horwath HTL
15 Scotts Road,
#08-10/11, Thong Teck Building,
Singapore 228218, Singapore
Tel: (65) 6735 1886
Email: singapore@horwathhtl.com

THAILAND / 泰国

Horwath HTL - Health & Wellness
37/10 Soi Langsuan,
Phloen Chit Road Lumpini,
Pathumwan Bangkok 10330, Thailand
Tel: (66) 2252 6281
Email: mbrennan@horwathhtl.com

责任编辑：王　军
美术设计：陈　芒
后期制作：肖俊卿

图书在版编目（CIP）数据

2023中国饭店业务统计 ：汉英对照 / 中国旅游饭店业协会，浩华管理顾问公司编. -- 北京 ：中国旅游出版社，2023.9
ISBN 978-7-5032-7198-4

Ⅰ. ①2… Ⅱ. ①中… ②浩… Ⅲ. ①饭店－商业经营－统计资料－中国－2023－汉、英 Ⅳ. ①F719.2-66

中国国家版本馆CIP数据核字（2023）第158962号

书　　名：2023 中国饭店业务统计

作　　者：中国旅游饭店业协会　浩华管理顾问公司　编
出版发行：中国旅游出版社
（北京静安东里6号　邮编：100028）
http://www.cttp.net.cn　E-mail:cttp@mct.gov.cn
营销中心电话：010-57377103，010-57377106
读者服务部电话：010-57377107
印　　刷：北京市青云兴业印刷有限公司
版　　次：2023年9月第1版　2023年9月第1次印刷
开　　本：889毫米×1194毫米　1/16
印　　张：3.75
印　　数：4200册
字　　数：150千字
定　　价：500.00元
ISBN　978-7-5032-7198-4

2003

2004

2005

2006

2007

2003 —— 2007 五年合集

2008

2009

2010

2011

2012

2003 —— 2012 十年合集

2013

2014

2015

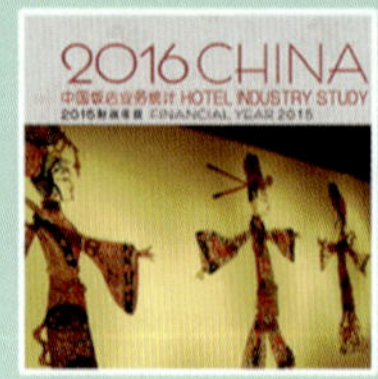

2016

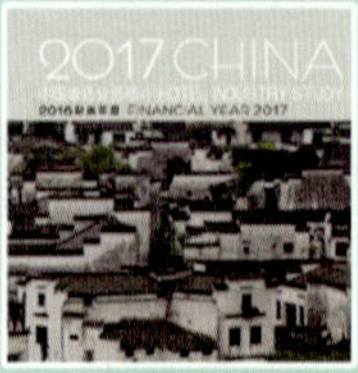

2017

2018

2019

2020

2021
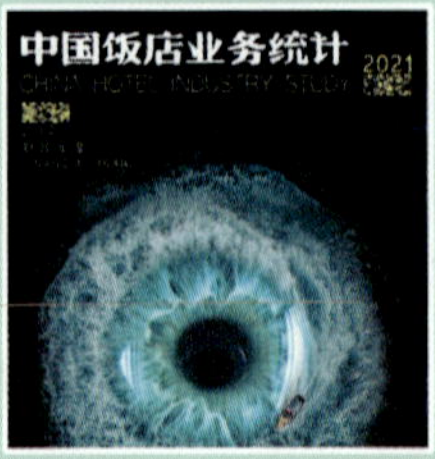

2022

2023年